MAGAZINE'S

Cycling for Health and Fitness

Use Your Machine to Get Strong, Lose Weight, and Feel Great

EDITED BY ED PAVELKA

RODALE

Cover and Interior Designer: Susan P. Eugster
Cover Photographer: Bob Allen/Outside Images/PNI
Interior Photographers: Mitch Mandel/Rodale Images, Paul Scraub, Chip Simons

Library of Congress Cataloging-in-Publication Data

Bicycling magazine's cycling for health and fitness : use your machine to get
    strong, lose weight, and feel great / edited by Ed Pavelka.
        p.   cm.
    Includes index.
    ISBN 1–57954–228–X   paperback
    1. Cycling.   2. Cycling—Training.   I. Title: Cycling for health and fitness.
    II. Pavelka, Ed.
    GV1041.B5275   2000
    796.6—dc21   99–056769

Distributed to the book trade by St. Martin's Press

    4   6   8   10   9   7   5   3   paperback

Visit us on the Web at www.rodalesportsandfitness.com,
or call us toll-free at (800) 848-4735.

RODALE

WE **INSPIRE** AND **ENABLE** PEOPLE TO IMPROVE
THEIR LIVES AND THE WORLD AROUND THEM

Notice

Due to the variability of materials, skills, and manufacturing differences, Rodale Inc. and the author assume no responsibility for any personal injury, property damage, or other loss of any sort suffered from any actions taken based on or inspired by information or advice presented in this book. Make sure you completely understand any procedure before beginning work. If in doubt, get help from a competent mechanic.

Contents

PART THREE

Stay Healthy

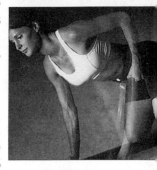

PART FOUR

Lose Weight

Introduction

This book is for all of you who don't want to race, ride centuries, or tour long distances (not yet, anyway). What you want right now is to use a bicycle as your means of reaching a higher level of health and fitness. You've picked the perfect vehicle, and you're holding a book that's dedicated to making your journey a success.

There's much to learn about cycling for fitness. You can improve by simply going out for rides, of course, but there are ways to get so much more from your time and effort. You'll find a wealth of how-to advice in the following pages, derived from experts who have made *Bicycling* magazine the leading source of health information for cyclists.

Heading the magazine's effort through the 1990s was Fred Matheny, *Bicycling*'s former fitness and training editor. Much of the advice you'll read is based on Fred's extensive research and coaching experience. He created the 30-member *Bicycling* Fitness Advisory Board that includes physicians, nutritionists, and health experts—all well-versed in the nuances of cycling. You'll receive guidance from these authorities throughout the book.

There is one risk in all of this, however. Once your program is underway and you are experiencing the fun and fitness that cycling adds to your life, it will be hard to resist moving up in the sport. That's when racing, riding long distances, and exploring your limits changes cycling from a recreation into a passion. If this happens, we have what you need next—the other seven titles in this collection from *Bicycling*. One, *Training Techniques for Cyclists*, should be particularly helpful. You'll find these guidebooks in bike shops and bookstores everywhere.

In the meantime, good cycling and good health!

PART ONE

Ride Right

1

How to Buy a New Bike

On one talk show, a consumer adviser was taking calls from budget-minded listeners. She discussed washing machines, computers, and automobiles. Her basic advice: Push for a discount no matter what you're buying.

Then came a call from a bike shopper, who said he had tried hard to get dealers to haggle, but no one would budge on the price. The expert was stumped and nipped the conversation short.

This is typical of how little most people (even consumer experts) know about the bike business. The fact is, selling bikes isn't like selling stereos—and visiting a bike shop is a lot different than visiting your local discount store.

Nonetheless, there are things you can do to ensure that you'll have a good experience when shopping for a bike. If you've decided to become a cyclist or to start riding more regularly as a way to improve your health and fitness, it's essential to have safe and reliable equipment. Today's bikes offer more features and performance for the money than ever before, making it a smart move to upgrade to a new model.

As you'll see, there are important advantages to buying from a professional bicycle dealer rather than a mass merchant. Expect to pay between $400 and $1,200 for a bike that will serve you well. The higher you go above the base price, the more features and less weight you get. You'll see bikes that cost more than $1,200, but for recreational riding, their refinements, though nice, aren't necessary. Save the money for the next great deal you find on a camcorder.

Here's a 10-point program for having a successful bike-buying experience.

1. Do your homework. Start by arming yourself with information about shops in your area. Talk with your cyclist friends and attend local bike club meetings. Riders will have recommendations based on their experiences. You want to do business with a shop that has friendly and knowledgeable employees, a wide selection of products, and a reputation for good service.

2. Pick a bike type. Narrowing your choice to one model can be
    daunting. Visit a shop and discuss your riding needs with a sales-
    person. A good shop employee will ask questions such as where you
    plan to ride (roads or trails), what you're looking for from cycling,
    and your price range. The three main bike choices are road bike,
    mountain bike, and hybrid—a bike that combines features of both.
    As you're deciding, take test rides on each of the three types so you
    can feel the differences in position and ride quality.

3. Try a specialty shop. Some shops specialize in one type of bike,
    whereas others carry an assortment. If you know what you want
    (say, a mountain bike with front suspension), visit a dealer who has
    made a name in mountain biking. Other shops may key in on road
    bikes or general cycling with emphasis on hybrids or even high-
    comfort, low-performance cruisers. If you're less certain about the
    best type of bike for your needs, stick with a shop that carries all
    varieties.

4. Don't expect discounts. Although you may find certain models on
    sale (usually at season's end), few shops can afford to slash prices.
    The reason? The average markup on bikes stinks compared to that
    of almost every other retail business. Hidden costs reduce profits
    and force dealers to demand full retail price. Bikes have high ship-
    ping costs, must be assembled, and usually come with a free
    checkup after the sale. These and other factors siphon from the
    bottom line until the dealer makes embarrassingly little on each
    sale. Of course, feel free to ask politely if the price is the best the
    dealer can do, but realize that demanding a discount may push the
    dealer's hot button. A better option is to ask for a discount on ac-
    cessories or cyclewear that you will purchase with the bike. The
    markup on these things is better, so some shops will work with you.

5. Include accessories in your budget. Don't go to your limit on the
    bike price before figuring in the cost of extra stuff you'll need. A
    helmet is a must-have item. So is a pump and tire repair kit. Cycling
    shorts are a key to comfort. You'll need a good lock if you'll ever
    leave the bike parked outside. Such items can add quite a bit to the
    total cost of a new-bike purchase.

6. Ask lots of questions. It's not uncommon for an expert salesperson to floor you with technical jargon that you don't understand. Don't simply nod your head and pretend that you're getting it. If the person assumes you are, he won't want to risk insult by talking down to you with elementary information. Make it clear that you are just getting up to speed with cycling. Don't be shy about asking questions. If the person doesn't have the patience to answer politely and thoroughly, go elsewhere.

7. Take a test ride. This is the best way to judge a bike. Make sure the tires are fully inflated, the seat is adjusted for your leg length, and the handlebar height is right. (The next two chapters focus on bike fit details.) If the bike has suspension, have the salesperson set it for your body weight. Wear the same clothes and shoes that you're used to riding in or will be riding in. Once on the road, shift and brake repeatedly. Climb and descend a hill. Make turns. If you're testing a suspended mountain bike, find rough surfaces so you can feel the shocks in action. Ride for as long as it takes to get a good impression of the bike. By testing two or three bikes this way, one should emerge as the clear winner.

8. Check out the service department. How shops handle service after the sale makes a big difference when your bike develops a problem. Most offer a free 30-day checkup that covers basic adjustments. Ask about ongoing guarantees on the frame and components. Some dealers have a convenient pick-up and delivery service. A shop should be proud of its service capability and eager to talk about it.

9. Don't overshop. It's common to throw up your hands and buy a bike simply because you are sick of shopping. But that's okay, and here's why: It's hard to buy a bad bike from a bike shop (as opposed to a department store). Although bike brands are distinct, all bike models at a given price are likely to have nearly identical components. This is because there are very few component makers. So once you narrow your selection to a couple of good bikes, it's silly to keep shopping. If you need a deciding factor, let it be your gut feelings about the shop and its employees.

10. Leave the mail-order catalog at home. Nothing irks a dealer more than seeing a discount catalog in your hand. The reason: They fear you're going to monopolize their time researching your purchase, then buy via mail-order to save a few bucks. Consider a shop's slightly higher prices to be an investment that earns you prompt service, expert advice, and friendly support for years of cycling enjoyment.

2
Road Bike Fit

No bike can perform to its potential—or let you perform to your potential—if it fits like a cheap suit. Fortunately, every bike model comes in a full range of frame sizes and allows several precise position adjustments.

If you're buying a new bike or you take your present one to a shop, experts can set you up with a comfortable, balanced, efficient riding position. Or you can do it yourself by using the information in this chapter. It's based on an interview with Ian Birlem, the owner of Pro Peloton, a high-end road bike shop in Boulder, Colorado. Birlem is so passionate about proper sizing that he won't sell a bike that doesn't fit, even if the customer requests it.

"Everyone has different cycling goals, flexibility, and needs," says Birlem, "and sometimes the general formulas don't work." As a result, he likes to put riders on a trainer and watch them in action. Here's the system he uses, plus steps for doing it at home with the help of friend. Work slowly and conscientiously to get the best position possible. Get used to the setup during several rides, then make further adjustments (if necessary) based on your body's feedback. Remember the first rule of bike fit: Adjust the bike to fit your body; don't force your body to fit the bike.

1. Saddle Height
Birlem begins by selecting a bike that's probably the size the rider needs, then mounts it on a trainer. He asks the rider to pedal easily and stop with a foot at the bottom of the stroke. Using a goniometer (angle-

measuring device), he measures the amount of bend in the knee. It should be 30 to 34 degrees. He adjusts seat height accordingly.

Do it yourself: Raise your saddle until your hips start to rock as you pedal. You can feel this, and your friend can see it from behind. Then lower the saddle just enough to stop the rocking. The result will be proper leg extension during pedaling, with sufficient bend remaining in your knees. Memorize the distance from the center of the crankset axle to the top of the saddle. Later, you can use it to quickly set your saddle height on other bikes you ride.

2. Fore/Aft Saddle Position and Tilt

With the bike in a trainer and the seat height set, Birlem has the rider sit centered on the saddle and stop pedaling when the crankarms are horizontal. He drops a plumb line (string with small object attached) from the front of the forward kneecap. It should touch the end of the crankarm. He slides the saddle forward or backward on the rails to get it right. Once seat height and fore/aft adjustments are correct, Birlem uses a spirit level to be sure the top of the saddle is horizontal.

Do it yourself: Have your friend drop the plumb line as described. After the fore/aft position is set, lay a yardstick lengthwise on the saddle

if you don't have a level. Compare the yardstick to something horizontal, such as a tabletop or windowsill. Tip: Some riders like to tilt the nose of the saddle down very slightly (1 or 2 degrees) to reduce pressure when riding in a low position. This lessens the risk of genital numbness.

3. Reach to the Handlebar

There's no formula for this. Birlem has the customer ride the bike for at least 15 minutes, making sure he or she feels comfortable and has no sharp bend in the back. "Most road bikes are set up for a stretched-out racer," notes Birlem. "But I suggest a more upright position that's obtained with spacers in the headset, a frame with a shorter top tube, or a stem with rise."

Do it yourself: While riding with your hands on the brake lever hoods, look down at the front hub. The handlebar should block it from your vision, or the hub should appear slightly behind the bar. If you can't achieve this with a normal 8- to 12-cm stem, you may need a frame with a shorter or longer top tube. Another gauge: With your hands on the handlebar drops, there should be about a 1-cm gap between elbows and knees at the closest point on each pedal stroke.

4. Frame Size

Birlem checks frame size after he has established seat position and reach. With these parameters set correctly, he wants to see 11 to 14 cm of seatpost sticking out of the frame. Also, the difference between the top of the saddle and the top of the stem should be 7 to 9 cm for racers and 0 to 4 cm for everyone else. If the frame is too small, it will be hard to raise the stem enough. Consequently, Birlem goes to larger frames with shorter top tubes to fit many of his customers.

Do it yourself: Use the straddle test. A road bike that provides about 2 inches of crotch clearance when you stand over it is in your ballpark. Unless you have an unusual build, you'll be able to position the bar and stem in their proper relationship.

5. Cleat Alignment

Birlem seats the rider on a table with the lower legs hanging down. He checks how the feet naturally align—toes pointed in, out, or straight ahead—then he duplicates these angles when he installs the rider's shoe cleats. Fore/aft cleat position is correct when the pedal axle is directly under or slightly behind the ball of the foot (widest portion of the shoe).

Do it yourself: Look at the angles your feet make using Birlem's method, and set your cleats that way. Then use several short rides to fine-tune the adjustment. (Carry the necessary wrench in your jersey pocket.) The goal is for your feet, ankles, and knees to feel neutral, not like they're angled against their will. Keep in mind that most current clipless pedal systems have some float, which allows your feet to pivot inward or outward several degrees before actually releasing. Position the cleats so your feet are in the middle of this range. The same technique works for off-road pedal systems, too.

3
Mountain Bike Fit

For pointers on setting up a comfortable and efficient mountain bike riding position, we turned to Troy Rarick of Over the Edge Sports in Fruita, Colorado. When he opened his business in the mid-1990s, this small town wasn't even a blip on the cycling radar screen. But by publicizing the area's pristine singletrack and promoting the Fruita Mountain Bike Festival, Rarick has made it a cycling mecca. His staff specializes in individual bike sizing using the following methods, swapping stems or seatposts until the fit is perfect.

1. Top Tube Length
For Rarick, this is the most important frame dimension. His rule of thumb: If your shoulder blades are drawn forward, the bike is too long. Conversely, if your back is hunched, it's too short. He makes appropriate modifications with the stem and handlebar, as detailed in these sections.

Do it yourself: Check your shoulder and back position in a mirror while riding the bike on a trainer.

2. Fore/Aft Saddle Position
Rarick sets the saddle by dropping a plumb line from the knee as described in chapter 2, but with one qualifier. Once he has the fore/aft position right, he wants to see the seat clamped in the middle of its rails so

there's room for further adjustment. "If you have to shove the saddle all the way forward, the seat-tube angle is too slack," he notes. (A slack seat tube—less than 72 degrees—places the rider farther rearward. Too far in some cases.) Also, the top of the saddle should be horizontal or tipped down very slightly.

3. Saddle Height

Mountain bikers tend to sit lower than roadies. This gives them more low-rpm power as well as greater agility on technical terrain. Rarick observes riders to be certain that there's still a significant bend in the knee at the bottom of the pedal stroke.

Do it yourself: Find the saddle height that eliminates hip rock (see chapter 2), then lower the seat another 3 to 5 millimeters to accommodate the challenges of off-road riding.

4. Handlebar Width

"Most bars are too wide," says Rarick, "so we use a hacksaw to cut almost every one we sell. But we never take off more than a quarter-inch

at a time. You can't put it back on if you make a mistake." Most standard (flat) bars are 22 or 23 inches—a good width for control and leverage, but too wide for tree-lined singletrack or a narrow, wind-cheating position. Most riser bars are even wider—25 to 27 inches.

Do it yourself: First, don't be in a hurry to cut down your bar. For recreational riding, a wider bar gives you surer steering and it also keeps your chest open for easier breathing, an important point if you have wide shoulders. If you do decide to perform this operation, it's not difficult. Most brake and shift levers can be loosened and slid inward. The best way to remove grips is to pry up the end with a screwdriver and drip alcohol inside. This will loosen them enough to slide off so you can use the hacksaw. To install grips, spritz the inside with hair spray. They'll slide on easily, then stick tightly.

5. Stem and Handlebar

With the correct frame size, a 120- or 130-mm stem should provide the right reach to the handlebar. "If you need a 150-mm stem to get enough, the top tube is too short," says Rarick. Two other factors affect reach: stem rise and handlebar type. Off-road stems vary in rise angle from 0 to about 10 degrees. A higher angle shortens reach, which also puts your back at a more upright angle. The upward bend of a riser handlebar shortens reach even more.

Do it yourself: Check your on-bike posture in a mirror. After a ride, soreness in your triceps indicates that your reach is too long, whereas discomfort in your upper shoulders means it's too short. With today's front-loading stems that open for easy bar exchanges, it's easier than ever to get your cockpit dimensions right.

6. Frame Size

"I like to see 7 to 9 inches of exposed seatpost," says Rarick. This tells him that the frame provides plenty of standover height for safety during sudden dismounts. Because most frames are now being designated simply as small, medium, or large rather than by a precise measurement, Rarick is much more concerned with top-tube length. He also keys in on the difference between the top of the saddle and the top of the handlebar, which should be between 0 and 3 inches. To check this, extend a yardstick or broom handle from the top of the saddle over the handlebar, then measure the gap.

4
Bicycling Basics

There's a lot to learn about the fine art of riding a bike. As cycling becomes part of your health and fitness program, lots of knowledge will come from experience. Meanwhile, how about a jump start? To help make cycling safer, more enjoyable, and more beneficial right from the start, here are the answers to eight questions most new riders ask.

Q: *How fast should I pedal?*

A: Most cyclists are efficient at 80 to 90 revolutions per minute (rpm) on flat terrain and 70 to 80 rpm on climbs. You can calculate pedal rpm, also called cadence, by counting the number of times either foot comes to the bottom of its stroke during 15 seconds, then multiply by four. An easier way is to use a cyclecomputer with a cadence function. If you can't pedal at these cadences, you're most likely using too large a gear. That's a great way to toast your leg muscles and injure your knees. You won't have much oomph left for accelerating, either. To learn to spin the pedals faster, stay in a lower-than-normal gear on gentle downhills and pedal up to 120 rpm, concentrating on relaxing so you can turn smooth circles. You've got it when you can spin this fast and your butt doesn't bounce on the saddle. Spinning at around 90 rpm gives your heart and lungs a great workout, whereas slogging at slow cadences wears you out before you get much cardiovascular benefit.

Q: *Where should I ride on busy streets?*

A: When cycling in town, it's tempting to get out of the way of overtaking traffic by riding as close as possible to parallel-parked cars. After all, you're supposed to ride as close to the right side of the roadway as practical. But by doing so you run the risk of being "doored"—crashing into a car door that's suddenly opened. To prevent that from happening, ride a door's width from parked cars (about 3 feet). You may have to make vehicles wait behind you, but a safe place to pull to the right probably won't be too far ahead. Keep the same distance if cars are angle-parked, because motorists may back out without seeing you. Always maintain a straight line past gaps between parked cars—darting in and out of empty spaces can put you right in front of unsuspecting drivers.

Q: *When drafting, how close should I be to the rider in front?*

A: Drafting is one of cycling's great pleasures. When you're riding in another person's slipstream, you can go at his or her speed while using about 20 percent less energy. The effect begins when you're within 3 feet. For recreational riding, that's close enough. It gives you room to maneuver in case of emergencies (potholes, broken glass, sudden braking, and the like). Also, don't ride directly behind the rear wheel. Stay a couple of inches to one side so you can see up the road. That's where you should be looking—scanning for anything that could disrupt the pace—rather than down at the wheel. Let your peripheral vision keep tabs on the gap. Elite cyclists may draft just inches apart at speeds of more than 30 mph. But such precision requires years of practice and plenty of trust.

Q: *Should I wear underwear with cycling shorts?*

A: No. The padded liner in cycling shorts (still called a chamois from the days when it was made of leather) is meant to be worn next to your skin. It's designed to absorb moisture while minimizing chafing. If you lubricate the liner with a product such as Chamois Butt'r, comfort increases. Do not use petroleum jelly, which clogs both your pores and the chamois material. The seams of underwear will only cause abrasions and the risk of saddle sores (not to mention unsightly panty lines).

Q: *Why do some riders start and finish so slowly?*

A: They've learned the importance of warming up before hard efforts and cooling down at the end of rides. Novices often hammer from the start, then get so blown 10 miles up the road that they plod home. Quick-starters also court knee injuries because they go too hard before ligaments and tendons are properly warmed up. Studies show that the body works at a higher level after about 10 minutes of low-level exertion in the chosen activity, compared to rushing into it from the gun. Start in the small chainring and spin with little or no pressure on the pedals. Cooling down is important, too. It allows your heart rate and core body temperature to slowly return to normal. Muscles are less likely to feel stiff if you end rides with 10 minutes of easy spinning.

Q: *How can I ride a straighter line?*

A: Riding a straight line keeps you safer in groups or traffic. But it's hard to do unless you learn to relax your neck, jaw, shoulders, and arms. Tension in any of these places means you're fighting the bike, and it will move jerkily from side to side rather than tracking dead ahead. Make a habit of looking 15 to 50 feet up the road (farther as you go faster). Staring right in front of your wheel guarantees that you'll take a wobbly path down the road. Practice your technique by trying to keep your wheels on the white line at the road edge. Also, ride rollers instead of a resistance trainer to develop balance and the smooth, even pedal stroke that keeps a bike tracking straight.

Q: *What's the secret to smooth pedaling?*

A: Seasoned riders have a fluid pedal stroke. In contrast, rookies are often said to pedal in squares, jabbing up and down without pulling back at the bottom or pushing over the top. To acquire what the French call *souplesse*, spend 10 minutes on every ride practicing a slow cadence of 50 or 60 rpm while applying only moderate pressure. Concentrate on pulling through the bottom of the stroke, as if you're scraping mud off the bottom of your shoe. Then pull up and forward through the top of the stroke, as if you're intending to touch the handlebar with your knee. Studies show that it's not possible to pull the pedals up with enough force to power the bike, but you can significantly reduce resistance for the opposite leg pushing down.

Q: *How can I cross railroad tracks safely?*

A: Tracks can cause a nasty spill if you don't handle them right. Slow down, stand slightly with the crankarms horizontal, and support your weight on your hands and feet. Reduce speed. Set up so your approach is perpendicular to the tracks. Cross at the edge of the road if you can because it's often less worn there. If the tracks are on a diagonal, you may have to look back for traffic and establish your right angle by swinging farther in the lane. Seesaw the bike with weight shifts as each wheel reaches a rail, reducing the impacts. If the tracks are wet or there's a metal sheet between them, slow even more and use extreme caution, or dismount and walk. Wet steel is like ice under bike tires.

5

Fast Fixes for Common Mistakes

Even experienced riders sometimes make rookie mistakes. What follows are 14 goofs that the *Bicycling* magazine editors continue to see when riding at cycling camps, centuries, and mountain bike festivals. But more important than learning what not to do is understanding how to do things right, so that's the emphasis here. No matter what kind of riding you're into (from road cruises to technical singletrack) you'll find tips to help you hone your skills, avoid common errors, and have more fun with less frustration as you gain cycling fitness.

Don't: Make sudden movements in a group or paceline.
Do: Keep your riding steady, smooth, and predictable.
Nothing disturbs a group more than a jerky rider, someone who makes abrupt movements that send ripples of fear through the paceline. One example: Instead of merely pointing out obstacles on the road, some riders yell, "Rocks! Gravel! Pothole! Dead skunk!" at the top of their lungs while waving an arm up and down at the offending bit of flotsam. Ride fluidly and predictably in all situations. Pacelines are an act of shared trust.

Don't: Ride on an aero bar in a group or paceline.
Do: Keep your hands on the brake lever hoods or handlebar drops.
Using an aero bar amid other riders is a major no-no for several reasons. First, you'll get yelled at. In some road circles, having an aero bar mounted at all is prima facie evidence that you have no group riding experience and probably shouldn't be trusted. The reason for this fear and loathing is simple: When using an aero bar, you're basically steering with your elbows and have a lot less control than when your hands are on the hoods or drops. If you need to brake for any reason, your hands are so far from the levers that you'll have to sit up abruptly to grab them, which takes precious time and could cause you to swerve.

Don't: Overgear on technical climbs.
Do: Pick a gear that lets you spin over obstacles.
It's tempting to bash through a tough section of singletrack in a big gear. After all, if you maintain momentum you can often skip over rocks

and roots that would stop you dead if you were going slower. That's fine if you're strong and skilled enough to pull it off, but once you bog down in a large gear, you're dead meat. That's why it's better to pick a gear a bit smaller than you think you'll need for a steep climb. Then when you encounter roots, rocks, or that 6-inch ledge you didn't expect, you can spin out of trouble rather than slogging to a stop.

Don't: Hammer every hill.
Do: Use your gears to keep your effort level steady as you climb.
If you have yet to ride with knuckleheads like this, don't worry, it'll happen—they go berserk on every hill, leaping out of the saddle and attacking, shattering the group's continuity and breaking everyone's legs. But by the last few miles they're usually so tired that all they can do is hang on the back. Their mission of disruption has been accomplished, however, because everyone has had a ragged ride thanks to their antics. There's a time to go hard on hills, but it's not when there's a cohesive group that's trying to maintain a steady pace. Save the heroics for your solo workouts or when riding with friends who agree that hill jams are the order of the day.

Don't: Stare at obstacles on the trail or road.
Do: Look exactly where you want your bike to go.
Have you ever seen a pothole or rock that you wanted to avoid—and then ridden right into it? There's a simple reason: A bike tends to go exactly where you look. If you stare at an obstacle, count on hitting it. Fighter pilots call this target fixation—they concentrate so intently on the target that they fly right into the ground. The same sort of thing happens to cyclists. The solution is to focus ahead on the line that takes you cleanly past what you want to avoid. The bike will follow your eyes, just like magic.

Don't: Stand up abruptly.
Do: Get out of the saddle in one smooth motion.
When you stand suddenly during a climb, your bike has a tendency to kick back several inches. This lurching motion can cause you to hit the front wheel of the rider right behind. If he doesn't crash, at least you'll scare him to death. When you regularly dropkick your riding companions this way, you'll stop being invited on group rides. To stand smoothly, shift one cog smaller (higher gear) than the one you're

climbing in while seated. As the next pedal comes over the top, smoothly rise forward without a hard jab that sends the bike back. Simply let your weight finish rolling the pedal around. The goal is a seamless transition to standing. Once you're up, resume normal pedaling.

Don't: Put your inside pedal down in corners.
Do: Put your outside pedal down and stand on it.
True fright is watching a novice rider totter through a corner with the inside pedal just millimeters above the pavement. If it hits, the resulting jolt will knock the rear wheel sideways, causing a crash. Here's how to eliminate this risk: Stop pedaling as you approach the turn. Put the outside pedal down (for example, the right pedal if you're turning left). Shift your weight to that pedal by standing so hard on it that you're barely touching the saddle. This puts your inside pedal up and out of harm's way, and it lowers your center of gravity so you can carve sharp turns with safety and style. Practice your technique by swooping around an empty parking lot.

Don't: Ride with a rigid, tight upper body.
Do: Relax the muscles of your hands, arms, and face.
The next time you're in a group, you might notice someone with white knuckles, locked elbows, a clenched jaw, and protruding neck veins. Or maybe it's you. Relax, literally. Think of your upper body as a form of suspension on your bike. Loose arms and shoulders absorb bumps on the ground as well as bumps from your group companions. If you ride with a death grip, those shocks get transferred to the front wheel and you could crash.

Don't: Accelerate when you reach the front of the paceline.
Do: Maintain the group's speed during your pull.
Pacelines are perfect when they proceed at a steady speed. But there's something about being at the front that makes riders want to hammer. Maybe it's the chance to show everyone how strong they are, or maybe it's the thrill of having a group strung out behind. Often it's simply a misunderstanding of how pacelines work. In any case, resist the urge to increase the speed. It'll make gaps open farther back, exhausting riders who should be getting an easier ride in the draft. Tip: When you're second in line, check your cyclecomputer to see how fast the group is

going. Then when the lead rider pulls off to drop back and let you through, simply maintain the current speed.

Don't: Let gaps open in a paceline.
Do: Keep a constant, close distance from the wheel in front of you.
If you're daydreaming in the middle of a paceline line and lose contact with the draft, you'll waste substantial energy catching back up—and so will everyone behind you. In fact, they'll be tempted to jump around you and conduct their own chase. Everything blows up. Stay alert and expend a little energy to smoothly close a 5-foot gap before you have to blow lots of energy bridging a chasm.

Don't: Overlap wheels.
Do: Ride 1 to 3 feet behind the rider in front of you.
Most crashes in packs or pairs happen when one rider overlaps the rear wheel of another. If the lead rider swerves or drifts, the trailing rider's front wheel can get taken right out from under him. Ouch. So always protect your front wheel. Think of it as your most precious possession when in a group. Nothing touches it. Nothing even comes very close. Your front wheel should spin along as if surrounded by an invisible force field.

Don't: Stare at the rider in front of you.
Do: Use your peripheral vision.
Pro road team coach Len Pettyjohn tells his riders, "If you stare at the rear wheel of the rider ahead of you, that's the last thing you'll see before you hit the pavement." Instead, keep on eye on that rider's rear wheel with your peripheral vision as you look past him to see developments up the road. The goal is to spot potential danger while there's enough time to safely deal with it.

Don't: Climb seated all the time.
Do: Vary your position and stand occasionally.
There's a trick to handling long climbs with minimal effort. It's simple and obvious—but for some reason many riders forget to do it. Simply alternate standing and sitting. If you never vary your position, the same muscles will get fatigued and your strength and efficiency will vanish. So sit for several minutes, then shift to the next smaller cog (higher gear) and stand. Rhythmically rock the bike side to side, letting your weight help push down the pedals. After a minute or so, sit and shift to a larger

cog—a lower gear that you can turn without the aid of body weight. Repeat the process all the way to the top.

Don't: Fight the wind.
Do: Be patient and smart when the gale is howling.
During much of the year, if you wait for a calm day you won't ride at all. Here's how to buck the breeze.

- Start into the wind. On an out-and-back course, do your hard work first while you're fresh and strong. Then you can spin back with a tailwind and work on your leg speed. It's better mentally, too, knowing that the ride's second half will be much easier.

- Don't overgear. It's natural to want to keep the speed you normally maintain on a given stretch of road in calm conditions. It won't happen. In effect, your usual gear becomes too big. Shift down but keep your cadence at its regular rate. This makes more efficient use of your energy and results in better training.

- Get low. Present as little frontal area as possible when battling a headwind. Get down in the drops or cup your hands over the brake lever hoods while resting your wrists on the handlebar. Use your aero bar if you're riding solo.

- Be strong mentally. A climb usually ends in minutes, but a headwind can last for hours. It's demoralizing because it's so relentless. Turn this into an advantage by telling yourself how much stronger the wind is making you and how good you're becoming in windy conditions.

6
How Much Should You Ride?

When Bernie Greenberg was in his mid-30s, he was working 80-hour weeks at his Denver law firm and training 2 hours every day. By the end of that season, he suffered from fatigue, heat intolerance, and vision problems. Eventually, he was diagnosed with multiple sclerosis. How could a healthy, hard-charging competitive rider suddenly become so ill? "Apparently it was a combination of racing and job stress, triggered by injuries from an earlier car accident," says Greenberg.

Can too much cycling make you sick? Did Greg LeMond's rare form of an even rarer disease—mitochondrial myopathy—result from an immune system pushed too hard by years of elite-level competition and the hunting accident suffered at the height of his career? More to the point for fitness cyclists, can lots of riding combine with typical life stresses to suppress the immune system, leading not to better health but to the colds, flu, bronchitis, and similar ailments that seem to plague amateur racers and even fast recreational riders?

Cyclists have asked such questions for years. The first scientific evidence hinting at the danger of riding too much came from a study of 17,000 Harvard alumni by Ralph Paffenberger Jr., M.D. Dr. Paffenberger found that the death rate was a quarter to a third lower among men expending 2,000 calories per week in exercise. But at higher levels of exercise—around 4,000 calories per week—the mortality rate rose.

Aside from this pioneering study, most conclusions about overtraining have been based on anecdotal evidence. Ed Burke, Ph.D., a professor and director of the exercise-science program at the University of Colorado at Colorado Springs, has worked with elite cyclists for 2 decades. He says he's become convinced that "chronic, hard, endurance training can depress the immune system. It isn't a healthy situation."

Hard Evidence

Until recently, there was little evidence of risks beyond the one landmark study and some educated guesses. Then came the results of a test performed in Poland. Fifteen young racers were examined, then rechecked after 6 months of intense training and racing (averaging more than 300 miles per week, much of it at extreme effort). Not surprisingly, ergometer tests showed marked improvement in their ability to ride stronger and longer. But lab work revealed a significant decrease in several immune system components. As they became fitter, their resistance to illness declined.

In Australia, researchers severely overtrained five male runners by subjecting them to two intense interval sessions each day for 10 days. After only 6 days, the runners showed significant reductions in the special types of cells that battle illness, as well as progressively declining amounts of body chemicals and substances that help prevent fatigue.

The message is clear. Riding too much or too hard can not only harm performance, but it might even threaten your health—and ultimately your longevity. The question is: How much riding is too much?

Moderation Means Safety

The same studies that reveal the harm of overtraining also demonstrate that moderate cycling doesn't weaken your immune system. In fact, most of the markers of a strong immune system are boosted by moderate training.

But defining moderation is tough because individual reactions to cycling vary greatly. A fast century might strengthen one rider's immune system while plunging other cyclists into illness. That's why professional racers are successful only if they have iron constitutions. The demands of high-intensity riding and lots of miles weed out racers with relatively weak systems.

Moderate cycling is also relative to the rest of your life. Pro cyclists can complete exhausting stage races because they think of little else but riding, eating, and sleeping. Their other needs are met by team support people, keeping their overall stress tolerable.

Consider typical recreational cyclists like Greenberg (or yourself). They train a fraction of the miles logged by a pro. But they often have demanding jobs, a family, maybe a stressful commute on crowded roads. No mechanic cleans their bikes. Is it possible to overtrain on 150 miles a week when pros routinely ride 500? You bet it is. In fact, when total stress is considered, many recreational riders may be working harder than the stars.

Cycling coach Tom Ehrhard agrees. "Stressors such as job, marital problems, or a poor diet combine with training to form a total stress equation," he says. "Keep this below your individual tolerance point and you'll be healthy and react to training by improving. Past your tolerance point, you're subjected to a fascinating array of sicknesses such as mononucleosis and chronic fatigue syndrome, as well as colds and flu."

Signs of Doing Too Much

So how do you know if you're going over the edge? Here are the signals of overtraining.

Poor performance. If your fitness worsens in spite of riding more, it's almost certainly getting worse because you're riding more. Take some time off, maintaining fitness with easy aerobic activities such as hiking or swimming at a heart rate below 70 percent of your maximum. Ehrhard recommends "putting a big cog on your cassette and noodling up hills instead of pushing." Although the rest that's needed to recover varies with individual riders, you might try scheduling 2 or 3 rest days each week when you resume riding.

General fatigue. Day-long exhaustion or lethargy is a sure sign. If you don't have the energy to mow the lawn, you have no business hammering with your cycling pals.

Negative emotions. A groundbreaking study in the 1970s by William Morgan, Ph.D., showed that the mood profiles of overtrained athletes are

Boost Your Immunity

Feeling overtrained? Here are five ways to fight the effects and manage the stress.

1. **Use antioxidant supplements.** Ken Cooper, M.D., who started the aerobics revolution in the 1960s, recently wrote a book called *Antioxidant Revolution*. Dr. Cooper contends that intense exercisers can produce free radicals in their bodies that damage their immune systems. (Free radicals are molecules that are unstable because they have one or more unpaired electrons. They try to stabilize themselves by attacking other molecules, damaging them when they steal electrons.) For cyclists who regularly exceed 80 percent of their max heart rate, Dr. Cooper recommends daily supplementation with antioxidants (nutrients that offset the negative effects) in these doses: 1,200 IU of vitamin E, 3,000 mg of vitamin C, and 50,000 IU of beta carotene.

2. **Reduce total stress.** Parts of your life seemingly unrelated to cycling can make you tired on the bike. "One of my riders was in the doldrums," says cycling coach Tom Ehrhard. "His job was bothering him a lot. I urged him to do something constructive. He not only looked into other jobs but confronted his boss. The boss was receptive and the rider felt like a huge weight had been lifted from him. And his legs came back."

3. **Adjust your goals.** If you have a demanding job and want to spend time with your family, don't aim for the Race Across America. Success in local events and club outings is possible with only 7 or 8 hours of riding per week.

reversed from those of normal people. Instead of being high in vigor and energy, overtrained athletes were high in anxiety, fatigue, and lethargy. Dr. Morgan commented that he'd never seen an overtrained athlete who wasn't clinically depressed. You don't need a psychologist to tell you when you're fried. Friends and family will usually let you know about personality changes. If you feel irritable and grouchy, short-tempered at work, and emotionally unstable, you could be spending too much time on your bike.

Vague physical complaints. "Sore throats or odd sicknesses can be leading indicators of chronic stress," says Ehrhard. So can sore muscles. Unlike impact sports such as running, cycling doesn't normally produce leg soreness. So if your gams are aching, you're overdoing it. Chronic diarrhea or heartburn can mean that your system is so overworked by riding that it can't process food properly.

Your goals should accurately reflect the time and energy you can invest in meeting them.

4. **Eat enough.** Overtraining symptoms are frequently due to chronic glycogen depletion, according to Ed Burke, Ph.D., a professor and director of the exercisescience program at the University of Colorado at Colorado Springs. And pay attention to a Japanese study that suggests sugar intake during cycling can enhance immune cell function. When cyclists rode at heart rates of 150 beats per minute and consumed a 25-percent glucose drink, their white blood cells were better able to respond to invading infectious organisms. (As a bonus, their endurance increased by a third.)

5. **Become more disciplined.** What? Isn't too much dedication what got you in trouble? Yes, but now we're talking about rest and recovery. According to coach Skip Hamilton of Aspen, driven cyclists need "tremendous discipline to go easy, especially when other riders sail by. You have to resist the urge to join them. You need to remember your training goals for the day."

A great way to keep easy days easy is to use a heart-rate monitor. Set the alarm to beep when you get within 50 beats of your max heart rate. If it sounds, immediately slow down. Or, simply stay in a gear so low that you barely feel pressure on the pedals. This is also a great time to ride with a friend who is way slower than you. Remember, easy riding in the pursuit of recovery is no vice.

Disruption of your normal sleep rhythm. Overtrained cyclists often fall asleep easily but wake abruptly in the early morning. Then at 10:00 A.M. they're ready for a nap. Poor sleep means it's time to reduce riding.

Elevated heart rate. It's useful to take your pulse each morning just after waking up. If you see an increase of 10 percent for several days, it probably means your body isn't adapting to the stresses of cycling.

An overpowering desire to buy a new bike. Don't laugh. Severe bike lust might mean you're no longer enjoying riding for the sake of riding. You could be bored and tired, subconsciously craving a different bike to provide freshness to your cycling.

7

Find Time for Cycling

Paul Robell, in his mid-50s, would never hold himself up as a cycling role model. He's a couple of pounds overweight and mending from a heart attack. He works 60-hour weeks at a job with financial responsibilities even Warren Buffett would find stressful. The demands frequently spill over to evenings and weekends. But despite it all, Robell manages to get out on his bike as often as five times each week, riding for better health and weight control. He's an enviable example of a rider who has a will and has found a way.

To anyone who whines, "I don't have enough time to ride," Robell will answer, "It's a matter of priorities. I may be too harsh here, but I think if someone says they can't find the time, they don't want to find the time. If you really want to ride, you can figure out a way to do it."

Which means it's a matter of creativity, too. Remember, you're not disadvantaged because you can't ride as much as you want, you're normal. Lack of time is the most common complaint among enthusiastic recreational cyclists. The trick to finding more is knowing a few effective strategies, then using your inventiveness to adapt them to your special circumstances. Robell's success hinges on one specific tactic— riding in the evening with lights on his bike, when necessary—and we'll add two dozen others that can jump start your imagination. Some are tips for finding more riding time, others help make the most of what you have.

The result could easily be enough extra time to double your cycling. But before you dive in, listen to another important point from Robell: "Even though I work at fitting in my rides, I'm less compulsive than I used to be. I've become much better at listening to my body. Occasionally when a long day drains my energy I don't ride even though I could. But I also have to remember that sometimes the hardest part of cycling is the first pedal stroke. Once I get out there I always feel better."

Ride early or late. With good planning it may be possible to ride before or after your core work hours, however long they might be. This is Robell's solution. As vice president for development and alumni affairs at the University of Florida in Gainesville, he's in charge of a campaign to raise $750 million. "My job is all-consuming and I work a lot of hours," he says. "But on the other hand, I always try my damnedest to make time to get some riding in." He needs to be at his desk by 7:15 A.M., so pre-work rides are out. He's usually able to leave at 6:00 P.M., making evening rides a good solution.

Depending on evening obligations to his work or family, he does this ride two or three times each week, then joins club rides on Saturday and/or Sunday mornings. "It's simply a routine," Robell says of the evening rides. "It takes just an hour and a half between getting off work and getting home to shower, and in that time I'm on the bike for an hour." He pencils these rides into his appointment calendar so they become as important as any other commitment—a good tip for everyone.

If your work hours are different, riding at dawn could be your salvation. It sets the tone for a confident day. You'll feel good about having your workout behind you, no matter what else happens. With modern bright and reliable street lighting systems, cycling no longer is a daylight-only sport. Lights create lots of time to ride.

Emphasize quality. Get maximum results from each minute on the bike by riding with a purpose. For example, if you're going with a group, practice your paceline skills. If you're solo, do low-gear sprints to work on your spin or climb hills to develop power. On a recovery ride, practice cornering, riding with no hands, or other skills that don't tax your cardiovascular system.

Know your needs. Let's say your goal is the club century. You may assume you need to be doing time-consuming 80-mile rides to train for it. Not true. Most cyclists find that they can quite comfortably ride about three times the duration of their average training ride, as long as they maintain a sensible pace, keep eating and drinking, and take an occasional break. If you find the time to average 35 miles every other day for several weeks, you should be capable of a 100-miler.

Ride hills. It's hard to beat the benefits of time spent climbing. Take it from three-time Tour de France champion Greg LeMond, who says, "There's no better training than riding hills. For me it was the easiest way to get in shape." It improves strength, power, stamina, and cardiovascular conditioning. As opposed to a flat 90-minute ride, one that includes a couple of thousand vertical feet will leave you feeling happily hammered, satisfied that you got a lot for your precious on-bike time.

It will also consume about 440 more calories if you're a 176-pound rider averaging 16 mph. Riders in this weight range burn 22 extra calories for every 100 feet of elevation gain, according to exercise physiologist David Swain, Ph.D.

Get into a routine. Keep your riding gear in the same place so you don't waste time hunting for something while your cycling clock is ticking. Lay out your clothes and food, and mix your drinks the night before. After the ride, put your sweaty clothes in the washer while you're in the shower. When you're clean, they're clean, and you can hang them to dry for the next ride. Routine means efficiency.

Drink your food. You want to go for a ride but you're famished. It'll pare pedaling time to fix a meal and eat it, then the load in your stomach will make you feel like human equivalent of a flat tire. The solution is to use a commercial drink that contains a calorie-rich mix of carbohydrate and protein. Scoop the powder into the blender with some skim milk and a banana for a nutritious and satisfying liquid meal. It takes less than 5 minutes and digests nearly as fast.

Ride inside. The point of this chapter is to find more time to enjoy cycling. Sweating for 45 minutes on an indoor trainer doesn't meet this definition for most people. It will, however, keep you pedaling when precious time for a real ride gets ruined by bad weather or life's frustrating little interruptions. Make the experience as interesting as possible by listening to music and/or watching cycling videos. Make it more productive by varying your pace with several surges to a high heart rate.

Merge one weekly ride. If you ride four times a week for 80 total miles, you can save time and probably improve your fitness by covering the same distance in three rides. The saving occurs because you have one less day of bike prep, dressing, warming up, cooling down, undressing, cleaning up, and so on. More on-bike time will be at a productive pace, and the longer outings will improve your endurance, too.

Ride less. That's right, less. If your attempts to wedge more cycling into your life result mainly in stress and frustration, relieve the strain by making rides 10 percent shorter. The pressure will disappear but your fitness won't if you increase ride quality. In the same vein, plan not to ride some days so you don't feel like you're being deprived. Use these days to recover from a tough ride or rest up for the next one. Take care of life's other responsibilities so time for cycling is both created and protected.

Forestall flats. For most of us, a flat tire costs about 10 minutes, a hefty chunk of time when you have only an hour to ride. Make punctures a thing of the past by using tires with a protective belt under their tread and/or installing an impenetrable liner. You can also use thorn-resistant tubes or add fluids that make tubes self-sealing. To save time when a flat does happen, use a CO_2 cartridge rather than a hand pump to inflate your spare.

Avoid incessant inflation. Some butyl inner tubes hold air pressure better than others, and all are superior to latex. By using less porous tubes, you can save time by adding air once every couple of weeks rather than before every ride.

Own a beater bike. How does an old-but-reliable bike save time? Because you can ride it on wet days and not feel like you have to thoroughly clean it afterward. In fact, it can save rides by getting you out the door in iffy weather. Install fenders, a rack trunk to carry wet-weather garb, and plenty of reflective tape. If all you have is a spiffy bike when rain is threatening, you can easily talk yourself out of risking a wet ride.

Own harsh weather gear. Just as a lighting system can create time for cycling, so can rainwear and winter clothing. Don't let a little moisture or windchill cancel any opportunities. If you have the right protection, you'll find that some very gratifying rides occur on days you could easily have stayed home to moan about the weather.

Become a mechanic. If you have the work space, basic tools, and know-how to take care of your bike's common mechanical needs, you can save lots of time. In just minutes you'll be able to fix a problem that would otherwise require two trips to the bike shop sandwiched around the several days your machine waits in line. Most problems are easy to remedy if you have a good manual. We're partial to *Basic Maintenance and Repair*, another book in this series from Rodale.

Be an instant fixer. Let's say you're on a ride and notice that the brakes need adjusting, a wheel is out of true, or the chain lacks lube. Service your bike immediately upon returning. You won't have to make time for it later or delay the start of your next ride—or realize in the midst of it that you forgot.

Use a dry chain lube. If you live in an area that isn't overly wet or humid, choose a lube that goes on wet but dries to the touch. The advantage is that you'll rarely, if ever, need to clean the chain or drivetrain to keep your bike working smoothly.

Attend a camp or tour. Want to add a week of pure cycling to your life? Do it on vacation. Camps are great because you ride every day and learn so much about training and techniques from experienced coaches. Tours let you ride to new daily destinations and stay in a memorable place each night. If you need incentive to find more time to ride, an upcoming camp or tour supplies plenty.

Get a coach. If you want maximum motivation to schedule rides and squeeze the most out of each one, hire a coach. Check at your local bike shop or club to see if there's one in your area. A list of certified coaches is also available through USA Cycling (719-578-4581; www. usacycling.org). Some coaches work with riders anywhere in the country through the mail or the Internet.

Tag-team babysit. Let's say that you have young kids who can't be left alone, and you know another cyclist in the same situation. Take turns babysitting the whole brood while the other person rides. This not only creates time for you and your friend, it can be something the youngsters look forward to.

Ride to family outings. You want to do things with your spouse and kids on the weekends, but you also want to ride. Do both by pedaling to the lake while the rest of the family drives. If you depart early, you'll all arrive at the same time, then you can enjoy the rest of the day knowing you got your miles. Throw the bike on the car rack and return with the family.

Ride a tandem. A bike built for two doesn't actually create time, but it does create time together. It's a great solution if your riding is reduced by concerns about leaving your significant other behind (either at home or way down the road). A tandem keeps two riders of unequal ability together and it makes chatting easier.

Tow your toddler. Rather than feel like a hostage to your youngster, put your bambino into a bike trailer made for that purpose and go for a ride. Besides creating on-bike time, you'll get a great power workout on hills. Look for a trailer that's weatherproof and has an anti-tip-over hinge. If your spouse isn't as strong but wants to ride too, the trailer will help equalize your speeds.

Ride at lunch. Many companies now accept noontime recreation by employees. Some companies even encourage it by providing lockers and showers. If you're able to snack at your desk, you can create almost an hour of riding by swapping your seat in the cafeteria for the seat on your bike.

Have a business conference. The reason sports stadiums have luxury boxes is because that's where corporations do so much business. In the same vein, if you learn that a client is a cyclist, that's a common bond that can help seal a deal. Invite that person for a ride, and turn a business meeting into a cycling opportunity. He will enjoy it as much as you do.

Commute by bike. We saved the best solution for last. Riding to work or school and back is still the best way to make time for cycling. Let's say you live 10 miles from your daily destination. Driving that distance in stop-and-go rush-hour traffic takes 30 minutes. By using a 12-mile route that keeps you off the busiest roads, you can ride there in about 50 minutes. So, you get 24 miles of round-trip cycling per day, and it takes only 40 minutes more than sitting behind the steering wheel, wondering where you'll find the time to squeeze in a ride.

PART TWO

Get Fit

8

10 Simple Ways to Improve Fitness

Simple? Improvement is supposed to be complicated. Intricate interval sessions, computerized training programs, heart-rate formulas worthy of Albert Einstein. Can you really get fitter without an advanced degree in exercise physiology?

You bet. You won't get raging fit without a plan, but you don't need a live-in coach, either. Try these 10 simple techniques for obtaining maximum fitness from the time you spend riding.

1. Follow a leader. You'll learn faster with a good teacher, so ask experienced riders if you can join them on their easy days. Watch how they corner or climb. Don't be afraid to ask for advice; most riders are happy to share information. Do a club ride and try to hang with the lead group for 5 miles. Next week, shoot for 10.

2. Fuel up. Have you ever stopped for a snack, then noticed how much stronger you rode shortly thereafter? Food is fuel, so keep your tank full. On road rides, perfect your ability to peel an energy bar or banana on the roll. And a midride picnic is an honorable mountain biking tradition.

Fluids are important, too. Adequate hydration combats fatigue and increases the distance you can ride. It lowers perceived effort and allows you to recover faster. Don't leave home without at least one big bottle of water or sports drink. You can improve your endurance by 30 percent with no additional training simply by packing in the fluid. Be a watermelon, not a raisin.

3. Lighten up. A few pounds can make a big difference in climbing performance. In a computer study, cycling researcher Chester Kyle, Ph.D., found that on a 1-mile climb reducing the weight of the bike and rider by 6 pounds produced an improvement of 22 seconds (nearly 300 feet). It can be expensive and complicated to lighten your bike, but it's easy to drop a few pounds from your body. Simply eliminate extra fat and empty calories by using the diet guidelines in part 4.

4. Unfold the lawn chair. Rest is almost as important as training. As you relax after an energetic ride, recuperation and improvement take place. According to Ed Burke, Ph.D., cycling physiologist and director of the exercise-science program at the University of Colorado at Colorado Springs, "It takes up to 48 hours after you've exercised to exhaustion to replenish the muscles' glycogen stores." Don't short-circuit this refueling process by riding long or hard again the very next day.

5. Ride slower. Most rides should be at a heart rate of 60 to 80 percent of maximum to ensure you're rested for the occasional hard efforts that stimulate improvement. Cycling coach Tom Ehrhard points out that the Australian national team, famous for gut-busting intervals, "spends 60 to 90 percent of its total training time at heart rates below 120."

   European pro coach Michele Ferrari notes that "most recreational cyclists tend to ride the same all the time—too hard on easy days and too easy on hard days."

   A slower pace burns body fat, increases aerobic capacity, and speeds recovery from harder efforts. On most rides, if you can't enjoy the scenery or talk with friends, slow down.

6. Use a heart monitor. *Bicycling* magazine's Fitness Advisory Board was nearly unanimous when asked the most important training device of the 1990s—the heart-rate monitor. But most riders strap one on only for hard workouts. Instead, says Dr. Burke, use it when you're going easy for recovery. Set the upper alarm at 75 percent of your maximum heart rate. When it beeps, slow down. Think of your heart as an engine and the monitor as a governor.

7. Bike on pavement and dirt. Although roadies and mountain bikers used to get along like two strange bulldogs, that's no longer true. Following the lead of the pros, nearly every serious cyclist has both types of bikes. Riding off-road is an easy way to improve your bike handling. It increases your climbing power and gives you a break from traffic-infested roads. Road riding builds endurance, improves aerobic fitness, and smooths out a pedal stroke made square by uneven terrain.

8. Enjoy other sports. Cycling is improved by cycling. But when the weather or your schedule preclude riding, don't flop on the couch. Instead, consider other sports. Running, for instance, is easier on rainy days or when it gets dark early. In-line skating relieves mo-

notony and uses many of the same muscles as cycling. An alternate sport also diversifies your fitness. If all you do is ride, sprinting for first base at the company picnic will make you sore for a week. Run briefly twice a week and you won't limp after beating out a bunt.

9. Ride like you feel. Periodization—carefully planning workouts for each day, week, and month—is an effective way to approach your training. But the pressure to complete a specific workout every time you ride can get old in a hurry. Most of us ride to escape stress, not to be consumed by it. So there's a lot to be said for setting aside the training plan and riding like you feel. Sprint for a road sign or a bluebird on a fence. If you feel great, jam a few hills. When you're tired, spin gently.

10. Befriend gravity. Choose a hilly route and improvement is simple. A stiff climb automatically strengthens legs and boosts your heart rate into the stratosphere. It's much easier to get close to your max on a climb than when riding on the flats. Great riders know this, and that's why so many choose to live in hilly terrain. Gravity simply makes you fit.

9
Condition Your Upper Body

Despite what your screaming quads may be saying, your upper-body pulling and pushing muscles (biceps, triceps, posterior deltoids, and latissimus dorsi) are just as important to cycling performance. With every acceleration from a stop sign or grind up a hill, you naturally pull down and back on the handlebar to counteract the pushing force of your legs.

Mountain bikers rely on these muscles even more than roadies, especially on those barely ridable climbs when they're bent forward, perched on the tip of the saddle.

Unfortunately, strong upper-body muscles don't come from riding a bike. Except during climbs or sprints, most of them are just along for the ride. That's why you need to do off-bike exercises. You'll become a stronger and more comfortable rider, and there's another bonus, too.

People will stop calling you "Rex" because of your bulging tyranno-saurus-like quads and twiggy arms.

These four simple exercises require only a light barbell, a dumbbell, door-mounted chinning bar, and 15 minutes two or three times a week.

Dumbbell Row

Hold a medium-weight dumbbell in your left hand. Bend forward at the waist, supporting your upper body with your right hand on a bench (see photo). Keep your back flat and nearly horizontal, like your position on the bike. Turn your palm toward your body. Let the dumbbell hang, then raise it to where your love handles would be (if you had them). Lower slowly. Do 8 to 15 repetitions, then repeat with the other arm. Do one to three sets.

Upright Row

Stand upright with your feet shoulder-width apart. Hold a light barbell with your hands about 4 inches apart, palms toward your body. Let the barbell hang from straight arms. Slowly raise the barbell to the level of your collarbones, letting your elbows flare to the sides. Lower slowly; do 8 to 15 reps. Be careful with this exercise if you've had shoulder problems—you shouldn't feel pain in your joints. Do one to three sets.

Dumbbell rows will build strong shoulders and arms.

Pullup

Everyone knows how to do pullups, and they're a great upper-body exercise. But if you don't have the strength to do many, or if they aggravate an existing injury, do them as "reverse pushups." Simply mount your chinning bar about 3 feet off the floor and lie face up underneath it. Grasp the bar with your hands a bit wider than your shoulders. You want your heels on the floor, your body straight, and your back slightly off the ground. Pull up until your chest touches the bar. Lower slowly to the starting position; do 8 to 15 reps. Do one to three sets.

Pushup

To balance your muscle development, finish your session with a pushing exercise. This strengthens your triceps, which are key to supporting your upper body as you lean on the handlebar. Dips are effective, but pushups are easier for most people because they can be done from the knees if the standard type (on toes) is too difficult. Lie face down and position your hands under your shoulders at the same width they are on your handlebar. Keep your back straight. Push up to full arm extension, then lower slowly. Repeat 15 times. Do one to three sets.

10
Leg Strength Simplified

Strong legs are a must for cycling. No surprise there. Resistance training helps develop leg strength that you can't get as quickly or as completely on the bike. The problem: Most lower-body exercises, such as leg presses or squats, require a trip to the gym or an investment in machines for your home.

Fortunately, there's an easier way. Here are three simple-yet-effective exercises you can do at home. All you need is a sturdy box for step-ups and dumbbells for added resistance. Each exercise is specific to cycling because it's done one leg at a time, just like the pedal stroke. We recommend 20 repetitions per set. Start with one set of each exercise, and shoot for three to five sets as you get stronger. Do this workout every other day, especially during winter or any other period when your riding time is reduced.

Step-up

Stand in front of a sturdy box that's 12 to 16 inches high. Put your right foot on the box, step up with the left foot, and then step down with the left foot. Repeat 20 times with the right leg on the box, then switch legs and repeat—that's one set. Sounds easy? It's not. When you get stronger, add resistance by holding a dumbbell in each hand.

Lunge

Stand erect with your hands on your hips and your feet shoulder-width apart. Keep your head up and your back straight. Step forward with the right leg so your thigh is almost parallel to the floor. Your right foot should land flat while the left foot rolls forward on its toes. Your right knee should be directly above the foot. Don't let your right knee sag toward the inside. Keep the left leg as straight as possible. Push back to the starting position. Remember to inhale as you step out and exhale as you return. Do 20 reps, then repeat with the other leg—that's one set. As with step-ups, add weight when you're ready.

One-Legged Squat

Balance on your right foot (see photo). If necessary, support yourself lightly with the backs of your hands or elbows on a door frame or one

One-legged squats are an unconventional way to build powerful legs.

hand on a chair back. Extend your left leg and rest the heel on the same box you use for step-ups. Or, bend your left knee and hold the leg behind you with toes pointed back. Keeping your head up and your back straight, squat down on your right leg until your thigh is almost parallel to the floor, then steadily go back up. As in lunges, don't let your knee get in front of your foot. Repeat with the left leg for one set. Hold dumbbells for additional weight.

11
Spice Up Your Riding

Dawn in the desert. A blood-red sun rising over an Arizona motel parking lot reflects off the jerseys of 40 cyclists shivering in the March chill. Race Across America legend Lon Haldeman is partial to early starts at his spring training camp in Sierra Vista, so some riders are making perfunctory efforts at calf-stretching and derailleur-tweaking. We're like restless cattle, eager to begin the day's ride.

But over to one side, a lone rider is prone on the blacktop, pumping out pushups, his breath coming in intermittent puffs of steam. He's Jeff Poulin, a software engineer from upstate New York. Pushups at 8:00 A.M. before a 75-mile ride? What's up with that?

"We all develop habits," Poulin says, "some good and some bad." He springs off the ground and climbs onto his bike. "So one morning I made a list of simple things to do every day—habits that will help my cycling and my health. Like early morning pushups.

"It's easier to change bad habits into good ones if you make changes slowly," he continues. "I try for one new behavior a week. And remember: You're trying to build a few good habits, not become a quivering neurotic, so don't worry when you backslide occasionally."

Using Poulin's good example, we came up with a list of beneficial cycling habits and advice on how to nurture them. Work each of these into your program and you're sure to become fitter and ride better.

On Your Bike
Warm up slowly. Do you jump on the bike and go hard from the start of every ride? Bad idea for your muscles, ligaments, and tendons.

Instead, begin in the small chainring, spinning gently at 90 rpm or less. If you use a heart-rate monitor, vow not to hit triple digits for at least 10 minutes.

Vary your efforts. Are all your rides the same? The cure is to choose a goal for every one. For instance, you can become a better sprinter by going all-out for the city limit sign each time you return to town. Or make it a habit to sprint at predetermined cues, such as every white mailbox. Poulin's cycling club does "yellow diamond" rides where they all sprint for road signs. "We have a blast," he says. "Sometimes we see signs far away and play cat and mouse. Other times they appear unexpectedly so we have a wild dash." These surges boost heart rate close to maximum each time, producing superior conditioning compared with steady-pace riding. Improving bike-handling skills can be another goal. If you have a mountain bike, ride it on trails at least once each week.

Learn to love hills. Many riders hate hills because hills make you hurt. But climbing also makes you stronger faster than any other type of riding. So include one hilly course per week in your regimen. In the process, you'll find the climbing style that works for you. Two former Tour de France winners make it clear that there is no one right way. Italy's Marco Pantani dances up climbs at a cadence of 80 to 90 rpm, whereas Germany's Jan Ullrich sits and grinds up effectively at about 60 rpm.

Master the minutiae. Are there certain small skills that you can't seem to conquer? Work on one each week until you have it mastered. For instance, if you usually fumble trying to get clipped into your pedals, concentrate on your technique at each traffic light or stop sign. Practice turning over the pedal and engaging the cleat until you can do it without even looking down. Do you always seem to lose ground to other riders going through turns? Find an empty parking lot and practice by carving around painted markings or paper cups that you set up. Practice other skills, too, such as reaching for your bottle, riding no-hands, turning to look behind, and so on.

Find a friend for motivation. If you sometimes lack motivation to get out the door, find someone with similar goals in cycling and ride together at least twice each week. "It helps you commit and it makes rides more fun," says Poulin. "My bike buddy and I ride at almost the same level but he likes to attack the hills and make me chase until my lungs explode. Then I try to get even on the flats until we finally call a truce.

It's made us both a lot fitter." If you don't know someone to ride with, join your local cycling club and you'll meet many riders.

Build your upper body. It's easy for cyclists to build buffed legs but still have wimpy upper bodies. To solve this, as soon as you hang up the bike after your ride, do a set of pushups, pullups, and crunches. Then slug down an energy-replacement drink to fuel your muscles for the next ride.

At Work

Stay hydrated. Do you swill multiple mugs of coffee as you toil in your beige cubicle? Instead, fill your mug with ice water. You can still make that sipping motion all day but you'll eliminate those caffeine jitters. And when it's time for your after-work ride, you'll be well-hydrated. The caffeine in coffee, on the other hand, is a diuretic. It actually promotes dehydration.

Walk whenever you can. Many of us phone our colleagues even though they're in the same building. Instead, walk over to see them in person. This stretches your legs, gets your heart beating, and burns some calories. For the same reason, always take the stairs rather than the elevator.

Sneak a stretch. There you sit, hunched over your desk reading those boring corporate reports. Instead, plop down on the carpet and do some stretching while you read. You'll find it more comfortable, and your alertness will increase, too. (You never know—there could be something important in there!) Other tips: Use a lumbar pad for your lower back, and position your computer screen to foster a more upright sitting position.

At Home

Ride and shine. Sometimes when we crawl out of bed, it can take half an hour to fully awaken. Get bright eyed in just 5 minutes by stretching lightly as soon as you roll out of bed, then doing 25 pushups and 25 crunches. Sure, this takes discipline to get started. But once you're in the habit, it's a relatively painless way to get in some quick upper-body work.

Do errands by bike. Chances are, you use the car too much. Instead, see how many errands you can do on the bike, such as going to the bank, buying stamps at the post office, or getting that bag of bagels at the corner bakery. If you're a tad shy about wearing spandex in public places, get some casual cycling clothes for these errands, such as baggy shorts and a logo-free jersey.

Stretch at TV time. Instead of vegetating on the couch while watching your favorite programs, flop on the floor and do your stretching. It won't seem like a chore when you're engrossed in a show. This is also a great time to massage your legs and work out any tight spots.

Take a bath. If your legs are sore from a long or strenuous ride, standing in the shower won't make them feel better. Instead, take a hot bath. It'll soothe your legs and relax your whole body.

Keep a diary. If you don't have a record of your rides and events, you won't know for sure which training has improved your fitness and which hasn't helped (or has even caused you to ride poorly). A diary doesn't have to be elaborate or take more than a couple of minutes to fill in. Note things like distance, time, terrain, average speed, weather, and anything unusual that may have contributed to the day's performance. Then give the ride a numerical or letter grade so you can see a pattern developing. Store the diary near your bike's parking place so you'll be reminded to keep it current.

12
Power Lunch

If you're looking for an effective way to make time for fitness every day, join the lunch bunch. Noon rides free your after-work hours for other activities and invigorate you for the afternoon droop that hits most people between 2:00 and 4:00 P.M. But is it really possible to fit a worthwhile workout into 60 minutes? Masters racer Dave George of Grand Junction, Colorado, knows it is.

Every day, George squeezes a training ride into his lunch hour with as many as eight of his coworkers. "During the season, it's plenty of quality training," he says. "And in the winter, it's enough maintenance so I can start riding more in February and be going well in a month. The ride makes our afternoons much more productive. It's a great stress reliever. It really changes your outlook."

Follow along with George and his friends. We promise to get you on the bike and back at the desk in 1 hour.

12:00–12:07

CHANGE CLOTHES

Grab your duffel and get changed. If your workplace doesn't have locker rooms and showers, use the restroom. Other possibilities are a private office, a janitor's closet, or a storeroom. Save time by packing your riding clothes so the items on top are what you put on first; for example, shorts, undershirt, jersey, socks, shoes. Some riders wear cycling shorts under their regular work pants so they can change quickly without baring everything (a ploy perfected by Superman). Save time by hanging your work clothes instead of folding them. Head for your bike. ("Walkable" shoes with recessed cleats make the journey easier and faster.) If the bike storage area is secure, you should have left your gloves, helmet, eyewear, and jacket (if one is needed) hanging from the handlebar. Put them on and head out.

12:07–12:15

WARM UP

Spin easily, increasing gearing and cadence every minute until you're moving at a pretty good clip. As you're doing this, you should decide what route you'll ride and be pedaling toward it. Ideal cycling roads might not unroll directly from your office door, but you don't need scenic splendor to stay fit. George chooses one of four main loops his group can cover in predictable times. (Out-and-back courses seem to work best for time management.) If the weather is bad, they stay close and do hill repeats. Another option is a training criterium on a 1-mile loop on quiet suburban streets or in an industrial park.

12:15–12:50

TRAIN

Crank away. George's group goes hard every day. "The rides are so short that we recover," he says. But listen to your body. Five days of intervals, sprints, training races, or hill jams might drain your energy and enthusiasm for weekend riding. (Afternoons at work won't be much fun, either.) If you need easy days, just spin and enjoy the fresh air.

Here are six workouts that cram lots of fitness into 35 minutes.
1. Do 15 minutes at time trial pace, 5 minutes easy, then another 15 minutes of time trialing.
2. Ride four time trial efforts of 5 minutes each, with 3 to 4 minutes of recovery between each effort.
3. Do hill repeats. Ride hard up a half-mile hill, then roll down easily. Repeat.
4. Build the pace into an all-out sprint every 5 minutes. Roll easily in between.
5. Do ladders. Go hard for 1 minute, then 2 minutes, then 3, 4, 5, and 6. Separate each effort with 2 to 3 minutes of easy spinning.
6. Team time trial. Trade pulls at the front of a fast paceline. Set a limit on time at the front, say 1 minute or 30 pedal strokes. This training works best with a closely matched group.

12:50–12:53

COOL DOWN

Three minutes isn't much time to cool off after a hard effort, so time your last interval to end with a 2- or 3-minute recovery. The total should be just enough to loosen your legs.

12:53–12:59

CLEAN UP

Stash your bike, head for the changing room, and strip. Save time by stuffing your cycling garb into the bag instead of carefully packing. If there's a shower, jump in and rinse off. If there isn't, use rubbing alcohol and a washcloth to wipe down. The alcohol removes odors and cools you enough to stop perspiration. The mission is to get presentable for possible afternoon meetings.

1:00

BACK TO WORK

George eats at his desk and sips a sports drink to rehydrate and replenish fuel stores. Or you can snack during an afternoon break.

Be careful: Lunch workouts can deplete your energy stores and leave you drained for afternoon work and evening activities. To stay alert (and employed), have a good breakfast. This is the meal that fuels a noon ride. Try oatmeal, skim milk, and a banana, along with a bagel or whole wheat toast. Then, at your morning break, munch an energy bar, bagel, or jam sandwich. Fruit is good, too. Try apples, bananas, or melon. In addition, keep a water bottle at your desk and sip all day.

13
Go the Distance

Long rides are a most excellent adventure for recreational cyclists. Maybe you can't time trial at 30 mph, ride the Tour de France, or win a mountain bike championship, but you can set a personal distance record. It's the challenge that almost every enthusiastic rider comes face to face with sooner or later. Part of the attraction is having so many opportunities. More than a thousand century rides—cycling's 100-mile classic event—are held in the United States each year. Most are organized by local bike clubs and represent the season's highlight for riders in their area.

To show you how you can make your cyclecomputer display its biggest mileage number ever (be it a quarter century or a double century), we enlisted cycling coach John Hughes, a Race Across America finisher and managing director of the Ultra Marathon Cycling Association. No matter what distance represents your personal fitness goal, Hughes knows how to get you there.

Get committed. "Begin by committing to a specific goal," says Hughes. "You can't be half-hearted and say, 'Oh, maybe I'll try a century sometime this year.' Once you decide on an event, do it—no second thoughts."

Of course, the commitment doesn't end with a promise. That's just the beginning. You need to pony up at least three training rides each week, the minimum to gain fitness and finish a long event. "Plan two endurance rides weekly of at least 2 hours," says Hughes. The third ride can be shorter and at a faster pace. Gradually build your mileage—but don't increase by more than 10 percent per week—until you can comfortably finish a long ride of 75 percent of your target distance. So, if you're shooting for a century, get in a training ride of 75 miles. "If you finish tired but excited about life and riding your bike, you'll be ready," says Hughes.

Don't use distance as your yardstick when training off-road. If you're preparing for an epic mountain bike event, work up to a training ride that's 75 percent of the total projected time, rather than distance.

Find the time. The biggest challenge for busy people is finding time to train. Search your schedule for available slots. Ride while the kids are at gymnastics or ride to your in-laws for dinner. Check chapter 7 for plenty of suggestions.

"Try commuting to work by bike 1 or 2 days a week," says Hughes. "Maybe you can make a deal with your boss. If you work longer on Tuesday, you can leave early another day to get in enough distance. Try to fit training into daylight hours—not after dark. It's riskier unless you're completely outfitted for night riding. You're better off on an indoor trainer. One exception: If you get up to ride early, it's safer because there's less traffic and there aren't many drunks on the road at 5:00 A.M."

Mirror the event. "It's easier to get out there with friends," notes Hughes. "However, training should mirror the event. If you plan to join pacelines in a century, practice pack riding. If you've challenged yourself to ride solo in a road event or you're planning a long off-road ride, get used to hammering by yourself in the wind. The same thinking holds if you've picked a hilly event—train on climbs. Also, practice things like changing flats, getting food out of your jersey pockets while riding, and eating on the move. You don't want any surprises on the big day."

Settle on equipment. "Go for gear that increases comfort rather than speed," says Hughes. "For instance, arrange aero bars to give you a higher, more relaxed position. Raise the stem and put risers under the armrests. Get everything dialed in halfway through your training period and don't change anything after that. Also, tailor your equipment choices to the event. For instance, install fenders if rain is expected."

Toting gear and food for long rides without suffering saggy-jersey syndrome can be a challenge. Put your spare tubes, patch kit, tools, and arm/leg warmers (if needed) in an under-seat bag. Then roll your rain jacket tightly and strap it to the outside of the bag. Balance heavy items such as sports bars by putting them in your jersey's left and right rear pockets. Save the middle pocket for light items such as lip balm, sunscreen, money, the route map, and your ID. Use a plastic bag to keep these items together and to protect them from sweat and rain.

Pace yourself. Before you toe the line, think about pacing. "Imagine how you'll feel at the halfway point," says Hughes. "If you ride the first half of the event as if you were already that tired, you'll have enough left to finish strong. Finding a paceline can make the ride more fun, but don't get in over your head. Ride at your own pace."

On the other hand, don't waste time. "Rest stops aren't for rest," he continues. "Don't sit down and eat. Instead, fill your bottles and stuff some food in your jersey pockets that you can munch on as you're rolling down the road. Spend 5 minutes, max, at any rest stop."

Tank up. Food and fluids are vital in distance events. "If you aren't urinating at least once every 2 to 3 hours, you aren't drinking enough," says Hughes. "And you'll need 300 calories every hour of the ride. Slug down energy drinks and eat sports bars, bananas, or cookies. If you don't eat enough, it'll get ugly." For unsupported off-road rides, carry enough water in a backpack-style hydration system to last the distance, or pack a water filtration device.

Ride in the present. A long event is just as much a mental challenge as a physical feat. "Divide the ride into thirds," Hughes recommends. "The first third you'll feel great, the middle third will drag, but the final third you'll be like a horse heading for the barn. If you realize that the middle part is mentally the hardest, you can overcome those feelings. Also, ride in the present. Don't worry about the last climb or how hard it will be when the route turns into the wind in five miles. Concentrate on the scenery, the act of riding the bike. Bargain with yourself: 'I don't have to finish the whole thing but I do need to get to the next rest stop.' Once you're there, set another goal for farther down the road."

Hughes saves his favorite tip for last: "In the final few miles of the ride, I spend all my time planning what I'll have for dinner," he says. "It's a great reward for accomplishing the goal."

14
Inside Cycling

Pedaling on an indoor trainer tends to get a bad rap, and why not? Sweat-soaked T-shirts, minutes that pass with purgatorial slowness, gasping for breath in air that smells suspiciously like your own perspiration. Only masochists and maniacs could learn to love spending time on the ol' vomitron, right?

Not necessarily. The key to making indoor riding more fun is, like anything else in life, variety. Spice things up and you'll start eyeing your trainer with longing rather than dread. Besides, an indoor spin solves most of your training dilemmas. It's time efficient: A great workout takes only 30 to 45 minutes because you're always pedaling, never coasting. It's uncomplicated: You'll never worry about darkness, weather, flat tires, traffic, or dogs. It's versatile: You can simulate almost any training scenario, including sprints, casual cruising, time trials, and even hills. And it's convenient: You don't have to clean grime off your bike, and you're within 50 feet of the nearest shower.

Now that you're convinced, let's key in on the all-important requirement: variety. Try these boredom-busting, fitness-boosting workouts that'll make certain your indoor training never feels like a route you've ridden too many times.

A 15-Minute Warmup

Use this before all trainer workouts.

- **Minutes 1–4:** Spin easily in a low gear (such as 39×19-tooth) at 60 rpm. Increase cadence by 5 rpm each minute.
- **Minutes 5–13:** Spin briskly at 90 rpm and decrease cog size by 1 or 2 teeth every 3 minutes (example: 39×19T, 39×17T, 39×15T).
- **Minutes 14–15:** In a moderate gear (such as 39×17T), spin fast for 10 seconds, then slowly for 10 seconds. Repeat.

Start Out Right

This is a great introductory jam session.

- **Minutes 16–27:** Start with isolated leg training (ILT). To do this, pedal with one leg and hook the other behind you on the trainer. ILT is an effective way to develop a smooth, round pedal stroke. Pedal moderately with the right leg for 2 minutes in a gear that allows about 60 rpm. Repeat with the left leg. Spin easily with both legs for 2 minutes. Repeat.
- **Minutes 28–37:** Ride briskly for 1 minute in a moderate gear at 100 rpm. Spin easily for 1 minute in a low gear. Repeat 5 times.
- **Minutes 38–43:** Alternate sitting and standing for 1 minute each. Stand in a large gear (such as 53×17T) at 60 rpm. Spin in a small gear at 90 rpm while seated. Repeat three times.
- **Minutes 44–45:** Cool down by spinning easily.

Climb Every Mountain

It's like riding the Rocky Mountains in your living room.

Setup: Elevate your bike's front wheel on a 4-inch block of wood to simulate a climbing position (see photo).

- **Minutes 16–27:** Ride briskly for 2 minutes, seated in a gear that allows 70 to 80 rpm. Spin easily in a low gear for 2 minutes. Repeat three times.
- **Minutes 28–42:** Ride briskly for 3 minutes, standing, in a gear that allows 60 to 70 rpm. Spin easily, seated, for 2 minutes. Repeat three times.
- **Minutes 43–45:** Cool down by spinning easily.

Boost Average Speed

Time trial to a faster cruising speed.

- **Minutes 16–21:** ILT. Pedal with the right leg for 2 minutes in a gear that allows about 60 rpm. Repeat with the left leg. Spin easily with both legs for 2 minutes.

Simulate a hill ride in your home.

- **Minutes 22–42:** Ride 5 minutes in a gear that makes you work hard at 80 to 90 rpm. Spin easily in a low gear for 2 minutes. Repeat two more times.
- **Minutes 43–45:** Cool down by spinning easily.

Visit the Pyramids

Reap quick gains from a tiered workout.

- **Minutes 16–27:** In a gear that enables you to maintain 80 to 90 rpm, do consecutive repeats of 1, 2, and 3 minutes. Spin easily between each for 2 minutes in a low gear.
- **Minutes 28–39:** In a gear that enables you to maintain 80 to 90 rpm, reverse the previous repeats (3, then 2, then 1 minute with 2 minutes of easy spinning between each).
- **Minutes 40–45:** Cool down by spinning easily.

Do Three by Three

Increase your power incrementally.

- **Minutes 16–42:** Maintain 90 rpm for 3 minutes in an easy gear (such as 39×19T). Every 3 minutes, shift to the next harder gear (smaller cog) until you can't sustain 90 rpm. Then reverse, shifting to an easier gear every 3 minutes.
- **Minutes 43–45:** Cool down by spinning easily.

Tricks on the Trainer

Use these workout tips to get even more variety and enjoyment on your indoor trainer without sacrificing any fitness benefits.

1. Ration your fun. In winter, limit trainer workouts to three per week, filling other days with cross-training activities such as running, weight training, skiing, inline skating, hiking, or swimming. This way you'll be fresh and eager when you do ride indoors.

2. Drink plenty. Keep your energy level high and avoid dehydration by sipping water or a sports drink throughout your workout.

3. Tune in the tunes. Indoor training is a great time to listen to upbeat music. When it rocks, you'll really roll.

4. View videos. Time goes faster if you have something to look at, so

check your bike shop for race videos or tapes made for indoor cycling.

5. Create a headwind. Body heat builds quickly without the normal air flow created by riding. Crack a window and position a large fan several feet in front of you. This way your energy goes into training rather than cooling your body.

6. Upgrade your cockpit. Put equipment on your handlebar that supplies useful information you can concentrate on. Get a rear-wheel sensor for your cyclecomputer (with cadence function) and use a heart-rate monitor.

7. Seek company. Inside cycling doesn't have to be a solitary pursuit. Resistance trainers are easy to transport, so consider inviting your friends to come for a "group ride" one evening each week.

15
Off-Season Training

In winter, bad weather and early darkness combine to deliver a powerful one-two punch to every cyclist. It's impossible to maintain on-bike training in most parts of the country, but doing nothing will destroy the fitness you built all summer. Studies prove that after about 1 month of inactivity, even the best-conditioned athletes lose most of their fitness.

Looked at another way, though, a shortage of cycling time after the autumnal equinox can be a blessing in disguise. If you continue to ride through winter, chances are great that you'll be mentally and physically tired when spring rolls around. So instead of moaning about winter, think of it as an ideal time to recharge your eagerness and develop the types of fitness that cycling doesn't provide.

With this in mind, here's the challenge: Emerge from winter with your fitness not only intact but improved, and your enthusiasm for cycling sky high. And do it all in a reasonable amount of time. Let's say you have 6 hours per week for exercise—4 days when you can devote

1 hour, and a fifth day when you can devote 2. Furthermore, because your time is limited, you can't afford to waste any of it commuting to a health club. All of your workouts must be done at or near your home.

As difficult as it may seem, there is a way to succeed even with such constraints. Here's how.

Winter Principles

1. Set goals. Know what you want to accomplish before you start. For instance, maybe you'd like to keep from gaining weight or even lose a few pounds. This would mean devoting a substantial portion of your winter training program to calorie-burning aerobic activities. At the same time, you wouldn't want to sacrifice any of your strength or cardiovascular capacity, so weight training and hill running might be in order. Whatever your goals, remember that for mental as well as physical reasons you may benefit from a break from cycling. This is a great time to experiment with other sports, but don't waste time on activities that won't help you reach your goals.

2. Schedule wisely. Assess your daily commitments to realistically determine when you can exercise. If you have a long lunch hour, you might be able to ride outside on mild days. If you don't have any free time until late afternoon, you may have to resort to inside cycling. Don't try to squeeze in workouts when time is too tight. This only leads to stress and frustration.

3. Keep it simple. Maintain your perspective. You're not training for the Tour de France. Your program doesn't have to be rigid or complicated. It should be enjoyable. And on a limited time budget, the simpler, the better.

Essential Components

1. Cycling. During the off season, de-emphasize cycling. You'll be that much more eager to ride come spring. But if you neglect the bike completely all winter, you'll acquire weak legs, a tender rear end, and an inefficient pedal stroke. The trick is to ride just enough to maintain your cycling fitness. In the dark days of midwinter, this means pedaling on an indoor trainer where it's warm and dry.

But even the most dedicated riders will find it difficult to ride inside a lot. One way to keep pedaling in easier-to-swallow doses is to use the trainer as a way to warm up and cool down from other activities such as weight training or running. This approach not only gives you the benefits of different activities, it also keeps your legs familiar with turning the crankset even though there's the all-important mental relief from cycling workouts.

Of course, if you can get out on the road occasionally, do it. But ride at a moderate-to-leisurely pace with friends (if possible), and make the main goal to have fun. If the sun is out but the roads are messy, try riding a mountain bike with fenders. The knobby tires provide good traction, and their higher rolling resistance gives you an ample workout even at slower speeds.

Take that mountain bike off-road, too, if conditions allow. You can improve your bike-handling skills, build power, and have a blast riding dirt roads and trails. When you get to sections too tough to ride, hop off and run with the bike. This uses different muscles and boosts your heart rate.

2. Resistance training. Cyclists need strong upper bodies to stabilize their riding position and reduce fatigue on extended treks. But riding by itself won't develop this type of torso. Resistance training is necessary, and winter is the ideal time to get strong. In keeping with our ground rules, here's what you'll need for an at-home winter weight training program.

■ An indoor trainer for your bike

■ A pullup bar

■ An inexpensive barbell set totaling 110 pounds

■ A sturdy bench

Begin each workout with a 15-minute warmup on the bike. Then do the following exercises. Choose a light weight—one that allows you to perform 10 to 20 repetitions without a helper. Begin with one set for each exercise. Add a second set as you get stronger, and add more weight when you can exceed 20 reps. If you're inexperienced in weight training, consult a book that shows how to do the different exercises correctly, or better yet, get professional instruction at a health club.

Pullup. In this day of fancy fitness machines, the simple pullup is still one of the best overall upper-body exercises for cyclists. It works the muscles that pull on the handlebar while sprinting or climbing. You can derive even more benefit by varying your grip on different sets—palms away, palms toward you, narrow grip, wide grip. If you're a real Tarzan and can do more than 20, tie a barbell plate to your waist for added resistance.

Bench press. This basic upper-body exercise strengthens the muscles that support your torso while riding. If your arms and shoulders ache during long rides, benches will help. But don't aim for heavy poundage. Use a moderate weight and concentrate on good form through the full range of motion.

Upright row. This exercise (see chapter 9) develops the trapezius muscles that help protect your neck in a fall. It also strengthens your shoulder girdle, thus guarding against collarbone fractures and shoulder separations. As a bonus, the added strength you'll derive from doing upright rows will help support the weight of your head and helmet on long rides, combating neck pain and fatigue. Use light weights for this one and don't cheat—keep your upper body still.

Pushup. This is another vital but unglamorous exercise. Pushups strengthen your triceps, the arm muscles that help support your upper body when you're leaning on the handlebar. Pushups are a good supplement to bench presses because they work the same muscles at a different angle. As with pullups, vary hand spacing.

Squat. This is the best exercise for developing leg power because squats work your quadriceps, hips, and lower back—the same muscles that produce your pedal stroke. Sometimes maligned as a cause of injury, squats are safe if you follow four rules.

■ Use light weights and do high repetitions (15 to 30).

■ Squat until your thighs are parallel to the floor, producing close to the same knee bend as when pedaling. Don't go lower.

■ Maintain correct form. Keep your back flat, your head up, and your chest out. Don't bounce at the bottom of the movement.

■ Stop one rep short of maximum if you don't have a helper. Otherwise, you could get stuck in the squatting position.

Crunches. This exercise builds strong abdominals. Though these muscles aren't used in cycling, they are crucial for supporting and aligning your back. If you experience low-back pain, especially on longer rides, crunches may be the solution.

End your weight workout by cooling down on the resistance trainer.

3. Aerobic activities. For variety and well-rounded cardiovascular development, cyclists should participate in other aerobic activities during the off-season.

Running is especially useful in winter. It's not only possible to run in adverse conditions, it's also easy to get a good workout in a relatively short time. In addition, running strengthens the calves and hamstrings—two areas that cycling overlooks. Hard uphill running, on the other hand, benefits the same muscles cycling uses.

Running has its disadvantages—chiefly the possibility of injury. To avoid being sidelined, invest in high-quality shoes with good support. On steep downhills, walk to protect your knees. And most important, start your running program gradually. You might begin by doing 4 miles this way: walk 2, run 1, and walk the last 1. Each time out, increase the running segment of the workout by a half-mile until you're trotting the full distance.

If you have access to a pool and the time to use it, swimming is one of the best total-body conditioners. You'll develop upper-body strength and flexibility as well as cardiovascular power. It's great for learning breath control, too.

Cross-country skiing and snowshoeing with poles are great fitness activities if you live where there's ample snow. In fact, the poling motion affords the same benefits as spending an equal amount of time in the weight room. If you're skeptical, just wait until you feel those tender triceps the morning after. Greg LeMond, the three-time Tour de France champion who lives in Minnesota, is a strong advocate, saying, "If you did a good ski program for 3 months and rode a trainer two or three times a week, you'd be ready to race with only 3 weeks of road training at the beginning of the season."

4. Other sports. No winter program is complete without including some fun sports to hone coordination and agility. Try the old standbys: basketball, volleyball, soccer, handball, and racquetball. Or go for more exotic activities like aerobic dance or karate. The more time you spend riding your bike in the summer, the more your basic coordination and agility tend to deteriorate.

Weekly Schedule

Here's a sample workout schedule for an average cyclist who works daily from 9:00 A.M. to 5:00 P.M. and also has family responsibilities. In keeping with the ground rules, this person has just 6 hours per week to exercise. This includes 1 hour 3 days a week after work when it's too dark to ride outside, another hour on Saturday morning, and 2 hours on Sunday.

Monday: Rest.

Tuesday: Spend 30 to 45 minutes running or doing some other type of aerobic activity. For the rest of the hour, ride the indoor trainer at a moderate pace.

Wednesday: Warm up for 15 minutes on the trainer. Do resistance exercises for 35 minutes. Cool down on the trainer for 10 minutes.

Thursday: Warm up with light stretching, jogging, or spinning on the trainer. Then participate in an active sport such as basketball. Cool down by walking or using the trainer.

Friday: Rest.

Saturday: Do any aerobic activity for 45 minutes, followed by 15 minutes of resistance exercises. Try one of the trainer workouts in chapter 14, or, if the weather allows, ride outside.

Sunday: If the weather is nice, ride for 2 hours at a moderate pace. In poor weather, combine activities. For instance, run for 30 minutes, do aerobics for 30 more, do a trainer workout for 45, then stretch and cool down for the remaining 15.

As the weather improves and the days get longer, devote more time during each weekday workout to cycling, and start adding miles to your Sunday ride. You'll be whole-body fit when the heart of the cycling season comes.

PART THREE

Stay Healthy

16
The Heart of the Matter

They carried him out in a black body bag, just like in the movies. Only this wasn't Hollywood, and he wasn't an actor. He was Joe Kita's father.

The coroner said it was a heart attack; nothing anyone could do. Age 61, recently retired. It's an unfortunate script that is played out every day in little square houses all over town. At least he didn't suffer, the coroner said, because it happened while he slept.

"I'm sorry, but there was nothing anyone could do."

In the months that followed, those last four words echoed in Kita's head like the bugle over Arlington. Part of it was anger at watching his father carried out like a sack of early-morning trash. Part of it was re-morse at never getting the chance to say goodbye or thanks, and really mean it. But part of it was simple, selfish terror—the midnight sound of that thick zipper closing—as if that were his genetic destiny, too.

It was this fear that finally pushed Kita into a doctor's office a year later for a complete physical exam. There the physician mentioned something that instantly made him stop feeling sorry and scared, some-thing so simple yet profound that he couldn't believe he hadn't realized it sooner.

"Your heart is a muscle just like any other," the doctor told him. "You can beef it up, or you can let it get scrawny and weak. You have that power."

You Have That Power

It's these four words that still echo in Kita's mind as he pedals along Pennsylvania farm roads in the early mornings when others his age are content in their slippers. There is something that can be done so he (and you) won't join the hundreds of thousands of men and women each year whose lives are ended by heart attacks. While cyclists often focus on crank-crushing quads or sculpted calves, all you have to do is realize, as Kita did, that the heart is not some mysterious, beating organ, but rather pure, powerhouse muscle. Such a subtle shift in perception will help you understand it better and enable you to target it with spe-cific aerobic exercises. Besides better cycling performance, you'll enjoy improved fitness, health, longevity, and overall well-being.

More Meat, Fewer Beats

At Kita's urging, *Bicycling* magazine—Joe, 39, is a former editor—developed a specific training program for heart health. But first, you need to understand how this mother of all muscles operates and the fascinating ways it adapts to endurance exercise such as cycling.

"When you hold a human heart in your hand, it feels like a piece of filet mignon," says Michael Crawford, M.D., chief of cardiology at the University of New Mexico Health Sciences Center in Albuquerque. "Only it's hollow, so it gives a little more when you squeeze it. But it's basically just muscle."

The heart responds to exercise the same way ordinary muscle does. Just as your chest expands with repeated bench presses, your heart grows with prolonged aerobic exercise. In fact, according to Dr. Crawford, a well-trained heart can be about 30 to 40 percent larger than a normal one. And since it's so big, it can pump about 50 percent more blood with every beat.

How to Train Your Heart

How can you be sure your cycling program is good for your heart while improving your performance and enjoyment at the same time? The secret is to mix up the type of training you do, because cycling at different intensities affects the heart in different ways. Essentially, your heart works in three zones of effort.

Easiest is an aerobic intensity of about 65 to 80 percent of your maximum heart rate (MHR), a pace that you can sustain for several hours. You don't need a heart-rate monitor to identify when you're in this zone. The effort feels easy to moderate and you can easily carry on a conversation. Second, and harder, is a pace that develops your lactate threshold, about 85 to 90 percent of MHR. It's an intensity that you can sustain for an hour or less. It'll feel hard. Duplicate it by time trialing 10 miles as hard as you can go for the distance. Third, your heart is capable of all-out short efforts that reach 100 percent of MHR. These develop your max VO$_2$, short for maximal oxygen consumption. This riding intensity feels Herculean.

A well-rounded training program hits all these bases several times a week. You have two choices. There's the low-tech method: You just ride and hopefully do enough at each level of intensity to improve. So in a typical week you'd cruise for aerobic work, do a time trial or an extended climb to raise your lactate threshold, and a couple of hard jams with friends would create max VO$_2$ improvement. Too haphazard for you? Then get a heart-rate monitor and follow this three-

These adaptations to exercise result in an ideal medical condition known as athlete's heart. It's what pro cyclists have—big, powerful pumps that fuel their superior performance. But while you may never be able to challenge the pros in a sprint or on a climb, you may be able to rival their hearts.

"You can demonstrate significant changes in heart size in 4 to 6 weeks," says Dr. Crawford, who has been studying the phenomenon of athlete's heart for 3 decades. "This doesn't mean that if you trained for 4 to 6 weeks you'd have the same heart capacity as someone who has been running marathons for 10 years, but measurable change will happen, even if you're a couch potato."

There are three specific, beneficial changes that occur in your heart with consistent aerobic conditioning, such as from cycling.

1. Your heart will get bigger. The heart weighs approximately 300 grams and is about the size of your fist. With the proper type of exer-

part training program to be sure your ticker gets the full range of effort each week.

- **Aerobic.** This is the easiest zone to monitor. Just spend about 80 percent of your weekly riding time cruising at a moderate but enjoyable effort, 65 to 80 percent of MHR. This is basic training for heart health.

- **Lactate threshold.** Get your heart rate into the 85- to 90-percent range twice a week for 10 to 20 minutes by riding the local club time trial or climbing a long hill. Or, do two or three repeats of 10 minutes each. Keep the effort steady and don't sprint at the end. Plan your energy expenditure so you feel like you could do one more repeat if you had to. The result will be a higher heart rate at which lactic acid floods your muscles and makes you slow down. You'll be able to ride harder or climb faster for longer periods.

- **Max VO₂.** These are the hardest efforts in your heart workout arsenal, but just a few minutes once a week pays big dividends in strength and power. After a good warmup, do 3 repeats of three minutes each at a pace so hard you can't last longer. This should push you to 91 to 100 percent of max heart rate. Roll easily for 3 to 5 minutes between repeats. Or, you can just jam hard and fast three times for a couple of minutes whenever you feel like it in the middle of an aerobically paced ride. Steep hills are natural for this.

cise, however, it can become slightly heavier and grow to the equivalent of almost two fists. (This is different from a so-called enlarged heart, which results from inflammation and is weak and diseased.)

"Because the heart is a hollow organ, there are two ways to make it bigger," explains Dr. Crawford. "One would be to just put more blood into it, stretching it out as if you were blowing up a balloon. The other would be to actually grow more meat. What happens in the athlete's heart is that it does both. It holds more blood, and there's actually more tissue there. It's just like when you pump iron and your biceps get bigger. The heart muscle grows as the biceps do, plus it dilates so it can hold more blood."

2. Your heart will pump more blood with every beat. To envision how this happens, think of a bicycle minipump. Now picture a high-capacity floor pump. If you pump both with equal force, which one is going to shoot more air into your tire?

Right, the big one. The same thing happens with an athlete's heart. Contrary to popular belief, it doesn't pump any more forcefully. Its larger chambers simply hold more and eject more, just like that heavy-duty floor pump.

3. Your heart will slow down. Because it's pumping out more blood with every contraction, the athlete's heart doesn't need to beat as often, especially when its owner is sleeping, resting, or simply involved in daily activities. The average American has a resting heart rate of 66 to 72 beats per minute, according to Paul D. Thompson, M.D., professor of medicine at the University of Pittsburgh. (Take yours right now by laying a couple of fingers alongside your Adam's apple for 30 seconds as you quietly read this, then double the count.)

By comparison, many well-trained endurance athletes have pulse rates around 40 when they awaken. Reportedly, five-time Tour de France winner Miguel Indurain's resting heart rate was a mind-boggling 28. Yours will probably never get that low, but it will decrease to a rate well below average as you become fitter.

The Advantages for You

Without a doubt, an athlete's heart is well-suited for elite-level performance, but how is it beneficial to overall health, and most important, why is it worth the effort of a consistent cycling program?

To answer this question, consider the experience of some monkeys who, in one ingenious study, had their heart rates controlled by pacemakers. Some were programmed for slower-than-normal pulse rates, and others were set for escalated ones. Interestingly, those in the first group developed less arteriosclerosis (thickening and hardening of the arteries) over time than those in the second group.

"Every time your heart beats, it creates turbulence much like a rushing river," explains Dr. Thompson, who is also director of preventive cardiology at the University of Pittsburgh Medical Center. "And turbulence in the coronary arteries creates eddy currents, flow differentials, and eventually maybe even arteriosclerosis. If you have arteriosclerosis, these arteries are like rubber hoses left out in the sun. Subject them to too much turbulence, and they can crack. This causes bleeding, clotting, and eventually a heart attack.

"I think a slow heart rate is absolutely beneficial for health," he adds. "In fact, there are about nine studies showing that the people with the slowest heart rates live the longest."

Possessing an athlete's heart can even extend your life in a more straightforward way. Greg LeMond, who won the Tour de France three times, was shot in the torso on a hunting trip during the height of his career. Like the proverbial Bible in a soldier's chest pocket, his meatier tissue may have prevented some of the shotgun pellets from rupturing his heart. He recovered to win two of his Tours after this near-fatal accident.

Beyond these advantages, a well-developed heart can also aid in recovery if you ever fall victim to a serious accident or disease. Sandy Beal, M.D., who operated on LeMond and oversaw his rehabilitation, suggests that his comeback probably wouldn't have been as swift or as complete had he not been so fit. "Without question, someone who is very healthy will tolerate an injury much better and, therefore, have less of a chance of problems and complications in the hospital," says Dr. Beal. "It probably contributed to his progressing and healing promptly."

So developing an athlete's heart is kind of like buying life insurance. And the required premium is regular installments of aerobic exercise. "It goes back to the basic physiology I talked about earlier," says Dr. Crawford. "For the heart to perform better, it has to get bigger, which means more blood must be sent back to it. You do this by moving the limbs to milk the veins of blood, push it back to the heart and thereby augment circulation."

What's Your Max Heart Rate?

The key to improving fitness is knowing your maximum heart rate, then riding at the specific percentages. The best way to find your max is to have a stress test or max VO_2 test in supervised conditions at a medical facility.

But with your doctor's permission, you can test yourself by using a heart-rate monitor and climbing a long, steep hill. Simply push until you think you can't go any harder, then sprint like the world championship is on the line. The pulse you reach will be very close to your max.

Beware of the old formula that says to subtract your age from 220. This can be wildly inaccurate. If it's off by eight or ten beats for you, the training formulas will make your efforts too easy for the best improvement, or so hard that you may become overtrained.

According to Dr. Crawford and Dr. Thompson, the sports that do this best, and consequently produce the finest athlete's hearts, are endurance cycling along with two favorite cross-training activities: rowing and cross-country skiing. Each of these activities recruits many different muscle groups, ranging from those in the upper and lower body for rowing and skiing, to the large leg and buttocks muscles in cycling. Unlike exercises such as weightlifting, where you're squeezing blood out to a specific working muscle but not encouraging much return, these activities create a veritable Indy 500 of blood flow in your body. Although any aerobic exercise will enhance circulation and benefit the heart, those that work a larger portion of the body achieve the most results in the shortest time.

Another reason that cycling, rowing, and cross-country skiing are so good for the heart is that they're nonimpact sports that can be done for long periods. "These athletes have such great hearts because they're able to train the most," notes Dr. Thompson. "You can train 5 hours a day on a bicycle, but there's no runner alive who can spend 5 hours a day running. It would beat the hell out of his joints."

17

Healthy Knees Guaranteed

Every year, *Bicycling* magazine hears from hundreds of readers with health and fitness concerns. What's the topic they ask the most questions about? Tingling hands, numb crotches, and ailing backs aren't even close. It's knees, knees, knees.

Ugly medical terms are associated with knees, words that sound like trouble when you say them. Chondromalacia, patellar tendinitis, medial synovial plica syndrome, pes anserine bursitis, IT band syndrome—a medical rogues' gallery of potential pain and misery.

Does this mean that cycling is hard on your knees? Far from it. In fact, it's the rehabilitation of choice for most knee injuries. Physical therapists know that when you can't run, walk, or hobble, often you can pedal a bicycle.

"Injured or surgically repaired knees want movement," says Andrew Pruitt, Ed.D., director of the Boulder Center for Sports Medicine in Boulder, Colorado, "and you want to exercise. They come together on the bike."

Still, knee injuries are an occasional fact of cycling life. "The cycling knee is unique," explains Dr. Pruitt, "due to the number of revolutions it makes." At an average cadence of 90 revolutions per minute (rpm), a rider cranks out 5,400 strokes each hour or about 1.5 million in a 5,000-mile year. That's a lot of potential wear and tear on cartilage, ligaments, and tendons.

Repetition isn't the only villain. Your knee isn't a simple joint that pumps up and down in a linear, piston-like motion. Instead, Dr. Pruitt explains, "your knee rolls, glides, and rotates" in several planes during a single pedal stroke. While cycling, your leg is anchored at the bottom by your foot, which is joined to the pedal by a rigid shoe. At the top is the massive bone and ligament edifice of your hip joint. Your knee wants to move between these fixed points, and if this isn't accommodated by correct position on the bike and proper placement of your foot on the pedal, bad things happen.

Mountain biking, interestingly enough, is less hazardous to knees than road riding. It sounds counterintuitive; mountain biking involves

the sort of high-torque, low-rpm grinding that knee experts have
warned against for years. Think about muscling up a short, technical
climb. You're seated, grinding at 40 rpm one minute, then your cadence
drops to almost nothing the next as you get out of the saddle and push
hard to grunt over a rock. Yet, Dr. Pruitt argues, "road riding is more
dangerous because of all the repetitive pedal strokes in one position."
Off-road, you're all over the bike, but what looks ugly and inelegant has
protective value.

So how do you protect your precious knees so that 10 or 20 million
pedal strokes down the road your hinges will still be well-oiled? The key
is knowing what to do and what to avoid, both on and off the bike.

On-Bike Rules

Perfect your position. On the next group ride, watch how people sit
on their bikes. Some are balanced and comfortable. They look powerful
even when they're pedaling easily. Others make your knees hurt just to
watch them—too low, too far forward, squatting like a frog on the
saddle. Bad position isn't limited to neophytes. Even experienced riders
make position mistakes when setting up a new bike. And position sometimes seems to be a fashion statement—low and to the rear one year,
forward and high the next. Knees don't like the vagaries of style. They
prefer consistency.

In his work with the U.S. national cycling team, Dr. Pruitt has pio-
neered "dynamic bike fit." This means he fits the bike to a pedaling rather
than a stationary rider. With his computerized system, he can quantify
exactly what the knees are doing at different points in the pedal stroke.

Lacking such wizardry, static measurements can approximate your
proper position. See chapters 2 and 3 for guidelines, but remember that
you'll need to fine-tune based on your unique body. For instance, riders
with long feet and those who pedal with toes down usually require a
higher saddle. A helpful rule: A too-high saddle usually leads to pain in
the back of the knee, whereas a low saddle can produce injuries in the
front.

Align your cleats. According to Arnie Baker, M.D., a masters cycling
champion, "poor cleat alignment is the biggest source of knee problems." Because modern cycling shoes have stiff heel counters that hold
the foot rigidly, proper cleat alignment is essential even with pedal

stems that allow rotational movement, or float. Get your cleats positioned by a coach, cycling-knowledgeable podiatrist, or bike shop that uses a professional cleat alignment tool.

Dr. Pruitt recommends pedal systems that provide between 6 and 10 degrees of rotation before the foot is released.

Keep your knees warm. Pros routinely cover their legs in training when the temperature is below 65°F. That's a good guideline, but you'll often see recreational riders with bare legs on cold, windy spring days, and they don't necessarily get knee problems. As in all things physical, there's plenty of individual variation. Dr. Baker says, "I don't cover my knees automatically whenever it drops below 60°F and no scientific studies have shown that it's necessary, but I wouldn't discourage it."

Warm up. Ripping out of the parking lot in the big chainring and putting the hammer down on the first hill is a training ride tradition that ought to be gracefully retired. Your knees need at least 15 minutes of gradual warming up. Spin gently, think about pedaling circles, and get the blood flowing before making any strenuous efforts.

Spin. Look at videos of the pros in action. You'll be struck by the rapid and fluid pedal strokes of the best riders. Even while climbing or time trialing, activities that make weekend warriors labor at 60 to 80 rpm, pros spin quickly. Here's a great drill: Next time you climb a familiar hill, use a gear at least two teeth lower than usual. For instance, if you normally use 39×21T, try a 24T and spin. You'll probably reach the top just as fast, and your knees will feel better because the stress is less. As a bonus, your leg muscles won't burn so much and your heart rate may be lower.

Build mileage gradually. "Doing too much too fast is a common source of knee problems," says Dr. Baker. It used to be called spring knee—mild tendinitis just above the kneecap from riding too far on that first warm day. The standard recommendation is to increase your total mileage by no more than 10 percent per week.

Beware of change. Change has become unavoidable in corporate life, but your body prefers consistency. When you alter equipment or position, your knees may file a protest. Installing longer crankarms, for instance, or riding a bike with a wider or narrower bottom bracket can often precipitate knee miseries. Whenever you make a change, give yourself several rides to adapt before going long or hard again.

Spin, don't push. Shift frequently in order to stay in gears that you can pedal at 80 rpm or faster.

Don't grind up hills while seated. When the strain increases, stand as much as possible even if you're a more efficient climber when seated. The more you climb out of the saddle, the better you'll become at it—and the more your knees will thank you for it.

Use the correct orthotics. To remedy foot imbalances for cycling, you need the "front posted" type of shoe insert that extends to just behind the ball of the foot. The more common "rear posted" type for walking and running isn't helpful for cyclists because it positions the heel, not the part of the foot that bears the pressure of pedaling.

Off-Bike Advice

You need to protect your knees off the bike, too. The following rules, however, don't apply equally to everyone. Take squatting, for instance. Some people can do heavy squats in the weight room for years and never have knee trouble. Others get chondromalacia (cartilage damage on the back of the kneecap) from squatting to pull weeds in the garden. In applying these rules, know yourself, use common sense, and minimize the risks.

Don't squat or kneel unnecessarily. Squatting puts pressure on back of the kneecap, while kneeling pushes it into the femoral groove, possibly damaging the smooth surfaces.

Be gentle going down stairs or hills. Running downhill is particularly hard on knees. Even mountain runners, accustomed to steep descents, practice techniques that cause their quadriceps muscles to bear the brunt of the pounding.

Don't do full-range leg extensions. This favorite quad-building exercise really loads the kneecap as the leg goes back and forth from a 90-degree bend to straight. If you need to do leg extensions to strengthen your quads, limit movement to the final 25 degrees before your knee straightens.

Get expert advice. If you do everything that this chapter recommends but your knees still hurt, find a cycling-savvy physical therapist or orthopedist to diagnose and remedy the problem.

18

Banish Back Pain

If "Oh, my aching back" is the first thing out of your mouth after riding, it's time to fix the problem. Assuming your riding position is correct, most backache misery can be solved or at least greatly reduced by adding abdominal exercises and stretches to your daily routine. For expert advice, we went to Karin DeBenedetti, M.A., A.T.C., who heads up the Biomechanics Lab at the Boulder Center for Sports Medicine in Boulder, Colorado.

"Cycling is unique," says DeBenedetti, "because it requires abdominal strength but doesn't build it. Extensive cycling often actually deconditions the abs." This works against you, and here's why: To avoid back pain, your pelvis must be rotated forward to take pressure off the spine. For this to happen you need strong abdominals and loose hamstrings and glutes (buttocks muscles).

The good news? To get a stronger belly and happier back, take just 10 minutes a day, preferably after a ride when your muscles are warm and relaxed. If you follow this easy program you can begin feeling relief in as little as 2 weeks.

Go crunch crazy. Crunches are one of the most common exercises, but many people still do them incorrectly. Here's the right way: Lie on your back with your knees bent, feet flat on the floor, and arms folded across your chest. Leave your feet free, not hooked under something. Now, instead of throwing your upper body forward like gym-class situps, DeBenedetti says to "steadily raise your shoulders off the floor, starting from your ears and rolling up, vertebra by vertebra, as high as you can go. It doesn't matter if your shoulder blades actually clear the floor. Pause at the top for 1 to 2 seconds, then roll back down slowly. Relax completely between repetitions so you reactivate your muscles, then repeat." (See photo on page 70.)

This shouldn't strain your neck muscles. It's all in the belly if you do it right. An active person with low back pain should aim for 200 reps every day. (Yes, you read that right.) It's okay to divide them into two sets of 100. If you don't have back pain, do at least 50 crunches a day for prevention.

Target your abs
to rid yourself
of back pain.

Pull your piriformis. The piriformis is a small, pear-shaped muscle in each buttock. To stretch it, lie on your back with legs extended. Bend the right knee. Grasp it with the left hand over the kneecap and your fingers on the outside of the knee joint. Keeping your right hip down, pull your knee across your midriff to gently stretch the piriformis, hamstring, and butt. "You should feel the stretch deep under your glute," says DeBenedetti. Hold the stretch for 10 to 15 seconds, release, and repeat several times. Do the same for the left side.

Stretch your hams. Crunches and the piriformis stretch are sufficient for prevention. But if you already have back pain, DeBenedetti recommends stretching your hamstrings, too. Sit on the floor with your legs straight out in front. Place the sole of your left foot against the inside of your right knee. Start bending at the waist, aiming your nose at your right kneecap. Go down until you feel a light stretch in your hamstring. Hold for 10 to 15 seconds, then straighten up. Repeat several times. Do the other leg.

Warning: If you experience tingly sensations in either leg while doing this stretch, it may indicate a disk problem in your back. See your doctor as soon as you can.

19

Solutions to Saddle Sores

The all-purpose term saddle sore includes not only small pimplelike lesions but also chafing, bruises, ulcerated skin, and full-fledged boils. These things have transformed pleasant rides into medieval torture ever since the days of wool shorts with leather chamois. Old-time racers thus afflicted would line their shorts with thin pieces of raw steak to help minimize the pain.

Left untreated, saddle sores can become infected and require extended time off the bike. But you don't have to suffer perineal misery (or ruin a good sirloin) if you practice a few simple preventive measures.

Dress for success. It's doubtful that you'll still find cycling shorts with a real leather chamois when you go shopping. If you do, don't buy them. Several washings will rob the leather of natural oils and make perching on its crinkly folds as comfortable as sitting on a tortilla chip. Instead, purchase a high-quality pair of form-fitting spandex shorts with a padded, synthetic liner (still often called a chamois). Modern synthetics are softer on the skin than leather, and they wick moisture that could hasten the formation of sores—something their animal-based ancestors can't do.

Well-made shorts have a chamois sewn flat so the seams can't rub you raw. Make sure it's large enough to cover your full sitting area. Some liners are one piece while others are stitched from two or three pieces. Most men can be comfortable in any style, but women should go for a one-piece or a curved "baseball" cut that eliminates seams on the midline.

Use lube. Because friction is a major cause of saddle sores, lubricate your crotch and even the chamois itself with a product made for the purpose, such as Chamois Butt'r. Look for something that protects for the duration of rides, but avoid heavy lubes such as petroleum jelly. It can clog your pores and is difficult to wash out of the chamois.

Wash before and after. The nasty bacteria that cause boils love hot, moist environments—and nothing is quite as steamy as your hard-working buns, encased in tight-fitting black shorts on a hot summer day. Use an antibacterial soap and water on a washcloth to thoroughly cleanse your crotch before each ride. Afterward, scrub carefully in the shower and towel dry. Some riders then apply alcohol as a disinfectant, but this can be painful if the skin has been the least bit abraded. It also could dry the skin too much, causing irritation.

Always wear clean cycling shorts for each ride, even on a tour or bike camping trip where washing them may be difficult. Soiled shorts have more bacteria, of course, and they don't breathe as well as freshly laundered ones. And don't walk around after a ride with a clammy chamois stuck to your skin. Wash up and change into loose shorts that allow the air to circulate. At night, you can keep your crotch dry for hours at a time by sleeping in the buff.

Use medication. If you are prone to saddle sores, *Bicycling* Fitness Advisory Board member Bernard Burton, M.D., recommends applying a prescription antibiotic gel such as erythromycin after every ride. On a PAC Tour, a 3,200-mile transcontinental ride in 3 weeks, two cyclists used erythromycin religiously. Result? Not one saddle sore despite averaging 140 miles a day on bumpy backroads.

If you develop a raw area from friction, Dr. Burton recommends an over-the-counter product called Bag Balm, "developed to soothe a milk cow's irritated teats." Look for it at your pharmacy or veterinary store and cow those saddle sores into submission. "Bag Balm applied to irritated areas after your shower will usually clear up the problem overnight," says Dr. Burton.

Level your seat. Poor riding position can cause a bumper crop of sores. If your saddle is too high, you'll rock side to side across it as you reach for the pedals, irritating or even breaking your skin. The same can happen when the saddle isn't level. Tilted up, the nose rubs directly on the front of the pubic area as you lean toward the handlebar. Tilted down more than a degree or two, you'll continually slide forward, then push yourself back. The resulting friction can rub you raw. If you suspect that poor position is contributing, check yourself with the pointers in chapters 2 and 3.

Be sure your saddle is wide enough so that your weight is supported on your sit bones (ischial tuberosities) rather than by the tender tissue between them. Beware of saddles that have a domed top or lots of foam or gel padding. These conditions cause your sit bones to either be lower on the sides or to sink in. In either case, the center of the saddle presses harder into the crotch.

Take a break. You don't want to stop riding, but getting the pressure off a budding sore for a couple of days may save you a week or more on the disabled list by preventing it from becoming infected. "Continuing to ride on an abscess," cautions Dr. Burton, "could result in multiple infections, scarring, and the tendency for more of these lesions to develop, even without additional trauma."

Soak away boils. "Soak in a comfortably hot bathtub three times a day for 15 minutes to allow boils to come to the surface and drain," advises Arnie Baker, M.D., a masters racer. "Hot water increases blood circulation, allowing more of the body's healing factors access to the afflicted area."

Soften the ride. In Dr. Burton's estimation, "Riding a bike with rear suspension eliminates about 90 percent of saddle sores. Suspension seatposts also help. Suspension reduces friction because you stay in the seat rather than bouncing up and down on rough ground or pavement."

Emergency repair. Okay, you've obeyed all of the above advice but still sprouted a saddle sore—and the big ride you've planned for all year starts tomorrow. What to do?

Andrew Pruitt, Ed.D., who has served as the medical coordinator for the U.S. national cycling team , suggests applying topical xylocaine and padding the sore with a nonstick moist burn pad such as Spenco Second Skin. This will numb the sore for a few hours of riding.

In many cases, however, cycling is out of the question. Some boils must be lanced and the unfortunate rider given a course of antibiotics. Sometimes even more heroic measures are required. "When I had bad saddle sores, I continued training," reveals Dr. Baker. "But what I did was hill sprints and intervals—all off the saddle and off my sores."

20
What Ails You?

As with most active athletes who work out regularly, cyclists can experience a variety of discomforts. This handy guide will help you pinpoint your problem and select the proper remedy.

Hands

AILMENT: Numbness and loss of grip strength (ulnar neuropathy)

CAUSE: Excessive hand pressure on the handlebar

SOLUTIONS:

1. Wear cycling gloves with padded palms.
2. Install padded handlebar tape or softer grips.
3. Change hand positions frequently while riding.

Lower Back

AILMENTS: Stiffness, soreness, or pain

CAUSES:

- Leaning over the handlebar for extended periods
- Handlebar too low in relation to saddle
- Overly long reach to the handlebar
- Leg-length discrepancy

SOLUTIONS:

1. Stretch before every ride; vary your riding position by changing hand location and standing regularly; do crunches to strengthen the stomach muscles that support the lower back.
2. Raise the handlebar to within an inch of the seat height.
3. Install a handlebar stem with less extension. (When you're riding with hands on the brake lever hoods, your view of the front hub should be blocked by the handlebar.)
4. Put a shim between the cleat and shoe on the shorter leg, or have a podiatrist design an orthotic (shoe insert).

Eyes

AILMENTS: Fatigue, dryness

CAUSES:

- Overexposure to ultraviolet (UV) radiation
- Wind penetration and/or poor tearing

SOLUTIONS:

1. Wear sunglasses with shatterproof lenses that block 100 percent of UV radiation.
2. Wear wraparound-style sunglasses and/or use a wetting solution.

WHAT AILS YOU? **75**

Feet

AILMENT: A burning sensation or numbness in ball of foot

CAUSES:

- Tight shoes
- Hard plastic soles
- Tight laces or straps
- Improper cleat position

SOLUTIONS:

1. Wear cycling shoes large enough to accommodate the slight swelling that occurs on longer rides.
2. Install a thin cushion insole.
3. Loosen laces or straps at the first sign of foot discomfort.
4. Move cleats rearward so the ball of the foot is slightly in front of the pedal axle, reducing pressure.

Shoulders

AILMENTS: Stiffness, soreness

CAUSES:

- Riding with locked elbows
- Improper handlebar width
- Improper handlebar stem extension and/or height

SOLUTIONS:

1. Keep elbows bent and relaxed to absorb shock.
2. Install a handlebar that equals your shoulder width.
3. Raise the handlebar to within an inch of seat height; install a stem with the proper extension. (When you're riding with hands on the brake lever hoods, your view of the front hub should be blocked by the handlebar.)

Neck

AILMENTS: Stiffness, pain

CAUSES:

- Heavy helmet
- Stationary head position
- Riding position too low

SOLUTIONS:
1. Wear a lighter helmet that still meets safety standards.
2. Periodically tilt your head from side to side while riding.
3. Raise the handlebar or install a stem with a shorter extension.

Thighs (Quadriceps)

AILMENTS: Soreness, cramps

CAUSES:
- Exceptionally hard or prolonged riding
- Inadequate training
- Insufficient fluid replacement

SOLUTIONS:
1. Massage and easy spinning for recovery.
2. Gradually increase intensity during the season; don't increase mileage by more than 10 percent per week.
3. Drink at least one bottle of water per hour (more in hot weather) and use sports drinks that contain electrolytes, which combat cramping.

Buttocks (Glutes)

AILMENTS: Discomfort, chafing, saddle sores

CAUSES:
- Too little or too much saddle time
- A seat that's too narrow, wide, or hard
- Improper riding apparel
- Poor hygiene

SOLUTIONS:
1. Ride regularly to condition yourself to the saddle, but don't increase mileage by more than 10 percent per week.
2. Use a moderately padded saddle that supports you on your sit bones (ischial tuberosities) but isn't so soft or wide that it causes chafing.
3. Wear cycling shorts with a soft, absorbent liner (chamois).
4. Wash your crotch before and after every ride; apply a skin lube such as Chamois Butt'r before every ride; wash shorts after every ride.

Knees

AILMENTS: Stiffness, soreness, pain

CAUSES:

- Pushing too big a gear
- Increasing mileage too rapidly
- Improper cleat position
- Incorrect saddle height
- Insufficient clothing

SOLUTIONS:

1. Use gears no larger than you can spin at about 90 rpm.
2. Increase mileage and intensity by no more than 10 percent per week.
3. Position cleats to accommodate the natural angle of your feet, or use a pedal system that allows your feet to float to their natural position.
4. Position the saddle so each knee remains slightly bent at the bottom of the pedal stroke. If pain is behind the knee, lower the saddle; if in front, raise the saddle.
5. Ride in tights or leg warmers when the temperature is below 65°F.

Ankles

AILMENT: Tenderness at the back of the ankle (Achilles tendinitis)

CAUSES:

- Inadequate warmup
- Climbing in too big a gear
- Improper saddle height and/or cleat position

SOLUTIONS:

1. Stretch before riding; start rides by spinning easily in low gears.
2. Use lower gears for climbing and alternate sitting and standing.
3. Raise the saddle slightly; be sure the cleat position doesn't place the ball of the foot behind the pedal axle.

Hips

AILMENTS: Chronic soreness, contusion

CAUSES:

- Improper saddle height and/or leg-length discrepancy
- Pushing big gears
- Crashing

SOLUTIONS:
1. Adjust saddle height so hips don't have to rock side to side to help you reach the pedals; put a shim between the cleat and shoe of the shorter leg, or have a podiatrist design an orthotic (shoe insert).
2. Use gears no larger than you can spin at about 90 rpm.
3. Apply ice periodically until swelling subsides, then resume easy riding to loosen the area and encourage blood flow.

Skin

AILMENTS: Sunburn, skin cancer; abrasions

CAUSES:
- Overexposure to ultraviolet (UV) radiation
- Crashing

SOLUTIONS:
1. Use sunscreen with a sun protection factor (SPF) of at least 15; cover burned areas with clothing to prevent further damage.
2. See a doctor about suspicious lesions or moles.
3. Clean wound thoroughly and cover with an antibiotic salve and breathable dressing; change dressing each morning and evening.

21
Fast Flexibility

Bob Anderson loves to ride, putting in 3 or 4 hours every day on his mountain bike in the hills near his Colorado home. He's also the Sultan of Stretch—the world's foremost authority on being lithe and limber. In fact, his landmark book, *Stretching*, has sold more than a million copies in nine languages.

But Anderson is a realist at heart, well aware that stretching is a hard sell to most cyclists, who wonder why they need flexibility. After all, your range of motion is limited to the circumference of the pedal circle or the reach for a water bottle. So why should you spend precious riding time on flexibility? There are several reasons.

Comfort. "Comfort is the key reason to develop flexibility," Anderson says. "It makes you feel better in the hamstrings, lower back, and shoulders. When you stretch, you'll feel less resistance while pedaling."

Flexibility. If you want to be able to use a low, aerodynamic position on a road or time trial bike, flexibility is crucial. *Bicycling* Fitness Advisory Board member Andrew Pruitt, Ed.D., says that you can't get truly aero if you can't touch your toes without bending your knees (before warming up).

Injury prevention. Limberness helps in a crash. "If you fall in an awkward position, flexibility will help you avoid injury," says Anderson.

Overall fitness. "You need to stretch because even if you're obsessed with cycling, you still do more than ride," says Anderson. "If you run, play other sports, or just sit at a desk all day, stretching helps protect you from injury and dissipates tension."

Slower aging. Hey, we aren't getting any younger. "Stretching helps as your muscles stiffen with age," says Anderson. "You don't have the same flexibility you did when you were 25. The goal is to be as flexible in 20 years as you are now."

Sold? Here are five preride stretches that Anderson recommends—and you can even use your bike as a prop while doing them. Although it's often said you should warm up before you stretch, Anderson thinks that the simple tasks of getting ready for the ride, such as dressing and pumping tires, provide enough aerobic activity to allow you to stretch immediately. For safety, do these stretches on grass or another nonslip surface if you're wearing slick-soled cycling shoes.

Calves. To stretch the right calf, stand 3 feet from your bike and lean on it, right forearm on the saddle and left hand on the handlebar. Step forward with your left leg, bending the knee. Keep the right knee straight behind you with the right foot about 18 inches behind the left. Slowly move your hips forward until you feel a stretch in the right calf. Keep the heel of your right foot on the ground and your toes pointed straight ahead. Hold an easy stretch for 15 seconds, relax, and repeat. Then stretch the left calf.

Quads. Stand beside your bike and hold the saddle with your right hand. With your left hand, grasp your right foot behind you and pull it up gently across your buttocks. Hold for 15 seconds, relax, and repeat (see photo on page 80). Do the same for your left leg. The knee bends at

a natural angle when you grab your foot with the opposite hand, so this
stretch also is good for problem knees.

Back and shoulders. Stand back from the bike and bend toward it.
Put one hand on the saddle, the other on the handlebar. Relax and keep
your arms straight and your feet directly under your hips. Bend your
knees slightly. Slowly move your chest down until you feel a gentle
stretch in the arms, shoulders, and back. Hold for 15 seconds, relax, and
repeat. When you come out of this stretch, save strain on your back
muscles by bending your knees more before standing.

Hamstrings. Lift your right leg and place the middle of the calf on the
saddle. Steady the bike with your left hand on the bar. Your right knee
should be bent about an inch. Your left knee should be slightly flexed
with your foot pointing straight ahead. Slowly bend from the waist, eyes
forward, until you feel a mild stretch in the back of your right leg. Hold
for 15 seconds, relax, and repeat. Stretch the left hamstring.

Shoulders. Raise the tops of your shoulders toward your ears until
you feel a slight tension in your neck and shoulders. Hold this feeling
for 3 to 5 seconds, then relax your shoulders. Repeat two or three times.

Stretching quads
can help with knee
problems.

22

Soreness Begone

As a certified massage therapist at Body Balance in Boulder, Colorado and a former world cycling champion, Eve Stephenson-Kiefel knows the benefits of a rubdown from both sides of the massage table. A pre-ride massage fires up cold, stiff muscles for the upcoming challenge. Postride, it banishes soreness and hastens recovery by increasing blood circulation.

Most cyclists can't afford the time or expense of regular professional massages, but there is an effective alternative, according to Stephenson-Kiefel: Just let your own fingers do the rubbing. Here's her quick and simple self-massage routine that will breathe new life into tired legs and help prevent muscle injuries. Get in the habit of doing it every day.

Start by applying a massage-specific lotion (available at health clubs or pharmacies) to your legs. Lie on your back on a bed or the floor with a pillow under your head. Then put your feet up on the wall (see photo on page 82). Inverting your legs like this during the massage helps blood drain from your muscles.

Start at your ankles, then move to your calves and quads using the three massage strokes listed below. Focus on the belly of the calf muscle, the outside of the quadriceps, and the glutes (buttocks). These muscles are so involved in the pedal stroke that they're susceptible to extra stress. They also need additional care, so come back to them after you've worked on other areas.

With practice, you'll be able to feel tightness at specific places in your muscles. Overworked areas will feel sore and painful to the touch.

Remember to always work up your legs from ankles to glutes, and make all stroking movements toward your heart. This technique pulls blood from muscles to improve circulation.

1. Begin with stroking to increase circulation and warm the muscles. With your fingers and palms, make long strokes from calves to quads on each leg.

2. Shake the muscles gently. Bend your knee and put a hand on either side of the calf muscle. Flop it back and forth like gelatin. Do this

Self-massage is great for reviving tired legs and preventing injury.

along the full length of each calf. Then do the same to the quads on the front of the thigh and the hamstrings on the back.

3. Knead the muscles between your hands like bread dough. Squeeze and compress, working out tight spots.

Because some body areas are hard to reach on your own, consider using massage tools. These are available at health clubs. Tools help you work on your back or glutes, for example. Even a simple tennis ball works wonders. Lie on your back, put the ball under your butt, and roll around on it, concentrating the pressure on sore areas.

23

First-Aid for Bike Crashes

On a postcard-perfect day, John Picone and his friends were ripping down Waterwheel Trail near Santa Cruz, California. Shrubs and bracken, nourished by recent rains, crowded the trail, forcing Picone and his posse to ride single file.

Picone was surprised when one rider sped past him just as they entered a corner. "She made the turn too wide," he recalls. "I saw her fly off the bike, straight for a tree. After she landed, all I could see was a big dust cloud and her feet. Thankfully, she missed the tree, but she was one big patch of crash rash."

More alarming, she was dazed and couldn't speak. Picone feared she was going into shock. Fortunately, one member of the group had brought a first-aid kit with enough supplies and had enough know-how to put her back together.

The lesson was well-learned: Picone now carries a first-aid kit every time he rides. He also brushed up on the medical-emergency savvy that every rider should know.

To help get you prepared for anything, here are 10 common cycling injuries and how to treat them. These expert tips come from Lyle J. Micheli, M.D., author of *The Sports Medicine Bible*, and Andrew Pruitt, Ed.D., director of the Boulder Center for Sports Medicine in Colorado.

Head or Spine Injury

THE FIX: Send for medical assistance immediately. Immobilize the head and neck. Watch for signs of shock (see "Heavy Bleeding and Shock"). Monitor the airway, breathing, and circulation. Provide rescue breathing or CPR as necessary, but only if you really know how. (Sign up for a CPR class by calling your local branch of the American Red Cross or the American Heart Association.)

WARNING: Don't move the rider or remove the helmet until a spinal injury has been ruled out. Any significant head or spine injury has the potential to cause death or permanent disability. Don't attempt to revive the rider using smelling salts because it may cause the head to jerk.

Loss of Consciousness

THE FIX: Call for help immediately. See if the victim is breathing and has a pulse (taken on the wrist). If the victim doesn't appear to be breathing, administer rescue breathing or CPR. Check for heavy bleeding (see "Heavy Bleeding and Shock").

WARNING: Do not move the victim until a spinal injury has been ruled out.

Heavy Bleeding and Shock

THE FIX: To control bleeding, cover the wound with a sterile dressing and press firmly against it with one hand. Elevate the injured area so it's above the heart. Cover the dressing with a stretchy bandage. If bleeding doesn't stop, squeeze the artery against the bone. For example, if the forearm is bleeding, squeeze near the biceps. For a leg wound, use the heel of your hand to press the front of the leg where it bends at the hip.

Shock is often associated with heavy bleeding and is potentially life-threatening. Symptoms include restlessness and irritability; altered consciousness; pale, cool, and moist skin; rapid breathing; and rapid pulse.

To reduce the risk of shock with any traumatic injury, have the victim lie down; control external bleeding; and elevate the legs about 12 inches (unless you suspect head, neck, or back injuries or broken leg bones). Maintain normal body temperature using clothing or a foil blanket to ward off chills.

WARNING: Don't provide food or drink because the victim should have an empty stomach if surgery is necessary. Also, it's much safer to wear sterile latex gloves before treating wounds.

Crash Rash

THE FIX: Flush the wound with water (squirts from a water bottle work well). With a sterile gauze pad and liquid soap, remove as much debris as possible to reduce risk of infection. Rinse again. At home, wash with antibacterial soap or soak sterile gauze pads with a solution of soap and water (one part soap to five parts water). Apply to the wound for 3 to 4 minutes at a time. Use a new soft-bristle toothbrush to gently remove remaining debris. Keep the wound moist by covering it with a bandage soaked in antibacterial ointment. Change the bandage twice a day until the wound heals (usually 7 to 10 days).

WARNING: Don't let a hard scab form. This will slow healing, promote infection, and could cause scarring.

Knocked out Tooth

THE FIX: Pick up the tooth by the chewing edge, not the root. Rinse it and place it back in its socket. Then place a piece of sterile gauze dressing directly over the tooth and bite down hard, keeping the gauze in place until you can get to an emergency room or your dentist. (If the tooth can't be retrieved, stem the bleeding by biting on the gauze until you receive medical care.)

WARNING: Don't throw away the tooth!

Dislocated Finger

THE FIX: Immobilize the finger in its dislocated position. Ice it for 20 minutes at a time as you go for medical attention.

WARNING: Don't attempt to realign the joint by pulling on the end of the finger to pop it back into place. The finger may be fractured. Attempts to fix the dislocation yourself can make the injury worse.

Broken Collarbone

THE FIX: Immobilize the affected arm in a sling and secure the arm to the body with an elastic bandage. Apply ice to the collarbone for 20 minutes at a time and seek medical attention. Note that broken collarbones and shoulder separations are sometimes difficult to distinguish in the field, but emergency treatment is the same.

WARNING: Don't attempt to ride for help on technical terrain with a suspected broken collarbone. Another fall could make the break much worse.

Exposure to Poisonous Plants

THE FIX: After encountering poison oak, sumac, or ivy, immediately wash the affected area with soap and water. Pharmacies carry products designed to remove the oils that cause the rash. If runny sores or a rash appear later anyway, make a paste with baking soda and water or use calamine lotion or hydrocortisone cream. All of these can help ease itching and discomfort.

WARNING: Don't put on garments that may have been exposed to the plants without washing them first in hot water. And don't take a bath after exposure, or you may expose other parts of your body to the plant oils. Take a shower instead.

Insect Stings

THE FIX: Remove the stinger by scraping it off the skin using your fingernail, tweezers, or a credit card. Wash the area with soap and water and cover it with a sterile bandage to keep it clean. If possible, apply a cold pack to reduce pain and swelling.

People who are severely allergic to insect stings may require rescue breathing. If you know you're allergic, ask your doctor to prescribe an EpiPen—a syringe loaded with epinephrine—which will arrest a severe allergic reaction. Carry it with you on all rides.

Emergency Supplies

To handle most on-bike incidents, here's what you need to take along for the ride.

☐ Adhesive bandages
  in assorted sizes*

☐ Adhesive tape*

☐ Antibacterial hand cleaner*

☐ Antiseptic ointment*

☐ Cell phone

☐ Cold pack
  (activates by squeezing)

☐ Elastic bandages

☐ Foil blanket

☐ Liquid soap*

☐ Sterile gauze pads
  in assorted sizes*

☐ Sterile latex gloves

☐ Scissors or knife, and tweezers*

☐ Snakebite kit (if you ride in an
  area that has poisonous snakes)

Items marked with an asterisk are found in the Cycle Doc first-aid kit, which is small enough to fit in an underseat bag or pocket. For the nearest dealer, call (800) 558-6614.

WARNING: Don't ignore the sting, especially if you may be allergic to insect bites.

Snake or Spider Bite

THE FIX: Snakebites are rarely fatal, but they should be treated as life-threatening. Wash the wound, keep the bitten area lower than your heart, and seek medical care immediately. If you can't get help within 30 minutes, consider suctioning the wound using a snakebite kit. If you suspect you've been bitten by a poisonous spider (including a black widow or brown recluse) or scorpion, wash the wound, apply a cold pack, and get medical help immediately. Antivenin is the only way to block the potentially life-threatening effects of the poison.

WARNING: Don't apply ice to a snakebite; instead, cut the wound in an attempt to drain the venom, or use a tourniquet.

PART FOUR

Lose Weight

24
The Need to Feed

In most recreational sports, eating is something you do afterward and, occasionally, beforehand. But in cycling, eating is often an important part of the activity. To most people who begin riding to improve their health and fitness (and even to lose weight), this is news. So, to bring you up to speed with the need to feed, here is quick primer on the topic—the why, when, what, and how of eating, drinking, and cycling.

Q: *Why do you need to eat and drink on the bike?*

A: Food replenishes the energy burned while riding. Every time you eat something, your body takes the food's carbohydrate (natural compounds known as starches and sugars) and stores it as fuel (glycogen) in your muscles and liver. You have enough stored glycogen to provide energy for 2 to 3 hours of riding. For longer efforts, however, you need to eat or your glycogen stores will become depleted. When this occurs, less fuel reaches your muscles and brain. You feel weak and dizzy, a condition known in cycling as the bonk.

To avoid bonking, nibble food if you'll be cycling for 2 hours or longer. Also, never leave home without plenty of liquids. Cycling causes fluid loss through perspiration and respiration, so you must protect yourself against dehydration, a major contributor to fatigue.

Q: *When should you eat and drink?*

A: The oldest advice for cyclists is still the best advice: Drink before you're thirsty, and eat before you're hungry. If you wait for your body to tell you it needs nourishment, the energy won't be able to reach your muscles fast enough to prevent a drop-off in performance. One rule of thumb is to take a big swig from your bottle every 15 minutes. You should consume about 20 ounces per hour, which is the amount in one standard-size bottle. (Drink even more if it's hot and humid.)

Another tenet is to allow yourself about an hour for digestion before riding. Then, if you'll be cycling for more than 2 hours, nibble periodically during the ride. During events, don't pig-out at rest stops. Your digestive system needs lots of blood to process the contents of a full stomach, which leaves less for your muscles. The result can be cramping and indigestion. So here's another piece of time-tested advice: At rest stops, stuff your pockets, not your belly.

Q: *What should you eat and drink?*

A: For fluid replacement on short rides, water works. But diluted fruit juice or commercial sports drinks are better, especially on longer outings. This is because they replenish energy-rich carbohydrate in addition to lost liquid. Drinks also are easier to ingest and digest than solids. According to studies, cyclists have the energy to ride nearly 13 percent farther when using a sports drink.

When off the bike, your diet should be 60 to 70 percent carbohydrate, 20 to 30 percent fat, and 10 to 15 percent protein. High-carbo foods include fruit, pasta, potatoes, rice, whole-grain breads, and vegetables.

Traditionally, the most popular on-bike food is the banana. It's easy to eat, provides about 100 calories of carbohydrate, and replaces potassium, an important cramp-combating electrolyte lost via sweating. Other fresh fruit, including pears (100 calories) and apples (80 calories), also provide carbohydrate, vitamins, minerals, and some fluid. And with the advent of so many varieties of energy bars, riders can choose their favorite taste and texture for a concentrated energy source. Most bars supply about 200 calories, primarily from carbohydrate, plus vitamins and minerals.

Some riders also do well on higher-fat foods. Fat is accused of being an inefficient fuel source compared with carbohydrate, but it provides a longer burn that seems beneficial on rides that last several hours. Experiment to see how fat works for you. One easy-to-use source is an energy bar that provides a 40/30/30 ratio of carbohydrate/fat/protein.

Many long-distance cyclists who ride at a steady, moderate pace mix nuts, raisins, M&Ms, whole-grain cereal or granola, and other favorite munchies into a personalized concoction called gorp (good ol' raisins and peanuts). This is easy to nibble, and doing so delivers a steady flow of food energy.

Caffeine (coffee, cola, tea) may give you a temporary physical and mental boost. It has been shown in studies to promote the metabolism of fat for energy. But caffeine also causes fluid loss through urination, and its beneficial effects for cycling are reduced if you are a routine daily user.

Q: *How do you eat while riding?*

A: The best place to carry food is in the rear pockets of your jersey. To reach it, first grip the handlebar with one hand close to the stem to hold the bike steady. Then reach back with the other hand to fish around for what you want. Rear pockets can hold an extra bottle, too. Put it or any other heavy item in the center of the three pockets so it won't tug the jersey to the side.)

Another approach is to snack during rest stops. It's common for touring cyclists to stash food in seat bags or rack trunks for roadside picnics. But as you now know, it's important to keep munching while riding between such stops.

Finally, don't forget the postride meal. As a cyclist, you'll regularly burn hundreds, if not thousands, of calories while exercising. So when you get home, you can guiltlessly enjoy an extra helping of your favorite food. In fact, eating a carbo-rich meal within an hour after finishing is the most effective way to replenish glycogen stores for the next day's ride. If it isn't practical to eat so soon, at least have another bottle of sports drink or one that's made for postexercise energy replenishment. Your muscles will thank you for it.

25
10 Keys to Better Nutrition

Here you are, determined to eat better and get fitter. Again. Chances are, you've tried—and failed—several times in the past. Such resolutions usually don't last because they contain words such as never ("I will never eat junk food again"), or they're much too general. Despite your good intentions, you set yourself up for failure even before you start. Instead, be specific and realistic. For example: "I will cut some fat from my diet by snacking on pretzels instead of chips." Rather than try to change everything at once, take small-but-effective steps that address one key aspect of your diet at a time.

With this in mind, here are 10 very doable suggestions that will help you eat better and ride better. Begin using them today and enjoy the results.

Drink enough on every ride. Studies done more than 50 years ago prove that maintaining hydration substantially improves endurance and helps prevent cramps. Unfortunately, too many cyclists take their bottles for a ride instead of drinking the contents. Drinking on the bike is a learned skill and requires practice. A trick: Set the countdown timer on your watch to go off every 12 minutes, and drink when it beeps. Your goal should be to finish every ride weighing what you did at the start, which usually means at least one bottle of fluid per hour.

Follow the "five-a-day" rule. When it comes to fruits and veggies, you should be eating at least five items each day. These food groups help prevent cancer, heart disease, and constipation while providing energy-rich carbohydrate. What a package! They're convenient, too—keep bags of scrubbed baby carrots, prewashed salad fixings, or fruit and vegetable juice in the fridge. To start, strive for five servings at least 5 days a week.

Eat breakfast every day. Believe it or not, people who eat breakfast extend their life spans and weigh less, according to a study conducted in California. And having something to eat before a morning ride extends your endurance. A good breakfast doesn't have to take much time, either. Try whole-grain cereal with fruit and milk, or a bagel with peanut butter and jam. Even a commercial meal replacement drink is a good start. If you're an avowed no-breakfast person, give this meal a try for 2 weeks. You'll see the benefits even if you're trying to lose weight. Studies show that breakfast-skippers tend to eat more total calories during the day.

Bone up on calcium. Bone health is maintained by the combination of calcium and weight-bearing exercise. Because bike riding isn't weight-bearing, cyclists need to pay close attention to calcium intake and add cross-training to their routines. How much calcium is enough? At least 1,000 mg per day for people under 50 years old, or 1,200 mg per day for those over 50. This means three high-quality calcium servings daily, such as milk, yogurt, cheese, or calcium-fortified products like certain cereals and fruit juices (check labels). Order a cafe latte, have hot chocolate made with milk at bedtime, or snack on low-fat ice cream to "bone up" on your calcium intake. Men: Remember that bone health isn't just a women's issue. You can get osteoporosis, too, so follow these calcium guidelines.

Eat on longer rides. You'll ride stronger if you take in some energy during the first hour and continue to do so throughout the ride.

Remember that the form can be solid (energy bars, cookies, fruit), liquid (sport drinks), or carbo gels. With gels or bars, make sure the wrapper can be opened easily while you're riding. Or, open the bars at home and rewrap them in wax paper before tucking them in your jersey. Depending on your body size, aim for 30 to 60 grams of carbohydrate per hour. (A typical energy bar contains 40 grams. Check the label.)

Cut the fat. Some of us still get more fat than we need for good health and good cycling. In a Danish study, men undergoing an 8-week training program made greater performance gains on high-carbohydrate diets than on diets high in fat. Cutting fat leaves room to increase your intake of performance-enhancing carbo. (Active adults should get about 25 percent of calorie intake from fat.) The key: Find specific, realistic changes that work for you. For instance, have your bagel with jam instead of cream cheese, or use mustard instead of mayonnaise on your sandwich.

Emphasize whole grains. Many riders follow the nutritional gospel of high-carbohydrate intake, but they don't emphasize the right kind. Your muscles may not be able to tell the difference between squishy white bread and crunchy whole-grain varieties (both provide fuel for cycling), but there's a big difference in their nutritional value. Whole grains win hands down, with more fiber, vitamins, minerals, and phytochemicals (for cancer prevention). So think "whole-grain" and "brown" when it comes to foods such as cereal, bagels, pitas, rice, and pasta.

Pop a pill. Taking a multivitamin/mineral supplement each morning probably won't make you a better cyclist, and it definitely won't fix a poor diet. But if you're already eating well it will make sure that you're getting enough folic acid, for example, which is important in preventing heart disease and birth defects. Despite a good diet, you may have an insufficient intake of certain nutrients, making a daily supplement cheap insurance.

Escape your dietary routine. Do you eat the same foods day in and day out? Even though bagels, peanut butter, bananas, pasta, and fruit juices are healthful foods, they don't make a healthful diet if they're all you eat. Make a resolution to try something you've never eaten before at least once each month—or better yet, once each week. For starters, try tongue twisters such as bok choi, tzatziki, hummus, papaya, gnocchi, pierogies, spaghetti squash, or calamari.

Don't stress yourself. Any self-improvement resolution, no matter how well-crafted, is doomed to failure if you become a slave to it. Remember, eating for health is more than individual nutrients and fat phobia. A healthful diet in an active lifestyle such as cycling has room for an occasional rich piece of chocolate cake. Look at it as a reward, not a failure.

26
Eat This Way

We live in a world piled high with calories at every turn—a glutton's dream come true. "Fast" and "convenient" are the mantras, whether we're talking about fast food, gourmet food, lowbrow hash and beans, ethnic eateries tempting you on the streets, the Twinkies and chips in your cupboard, or the packaged entrees stockpiled in your freezer. We're awash in nutritional choices. Finding the ideal diet, much less the time to prepare it, can seem an impossible quest. To help you through the dietary maze, here's a list of intelligent, quick, and easy meals with the reasoning behind each one.

This ideal dietary day is designed for a 40-year-old male cyclist who weighs 180 pounds and rides for an hour each day. He needs 2,700 to 3,200 calories daily, plus another 800 for his hour of cycling. A 130-pound woman should decrease the daily portions by 25 percent and eliminate the evening snack. If you're maintaining your weight and feeling energetic, you can be sure you're getting the right number of calories.

Breakfast: 7:00 A.M.

Toasted multigrain bagel with apricot jam

1½ cups bran flakes

1 medium sliced banana

1 cup fat-free milk

Total calories: 775

News headlines vary widely on how diet affects conditions such as heart disease, cancer, high blood pressure, and osteoporosis—but four nutritional constituents (fiber, low fat, fruits, vegetables) have withstood the test of time. In general, your diet should include at least 25 grams per day of fiber, obtained through whole grains, beans, and lots of fruits and veggies. These high-fiber foods are also low in fat, so eat up. They'll help reduce room for fat intake, which should be no more than 25 to 30 percent of calories. Plus, fruits and vegetables provide vitamins and minerals.

Snack: 10:00 A.M.

1 cup low-fat fruit yogurt

Large oatmeal cookie

Total calories: 400

To function well throughout the day, you need to eat and drink frequently. A general guideline is not to go more than 4 hours during the day without a bite. If you're up with the birds and eat a late lunch, you'll need a midmorning snack. If you train after work and don't eat dinner until you've ridden, showered, shopped for food, driven home, and pushed the buttons on the microwave, you should also snack in midafternoon. (Ideally, allow a couple of hours between eating and a workout to let your stomach empty and the nutrients to be absorbed.) One other benefit of snacking: You won't be famished at regular meals. You'll want less then, which usually means you'll eat fewer total calories every day.

Lunch: 1:00 P.M.

Black bean soup mix (add hot water)

Chicken wrap (large tortilla, cream cheese, salsa or hoisin sauce, large
    lettuce leaf, 2 ounces of sliced chicken, chopped raw cucumbers,
    tomatoes)

5 raw baby carrots

Orange

Rice Krispie–treat square

Total calories: 700

Meals should include at least three food groups and a variety of unprocessed foods to meet your energy and dietary needs. This meal has foods from the breads and cereals group (tortilla), fruit group (orange), veggie group (baby carrots, cucumber, tomato) and protein group (black beans, chicken). Remember: Taking a multivitamin/mineral supplement can help a good diet meet full nutritional requirements, but it can't make up for a substandard diet.

Snack: 3:00 P.M.

2 rye crackers

1½ oz. Swiss cheese

1 cup apple juice

Total calories: 325

Even moderate dehydration can lessen cycling performance, increase fatigue and leave you with a headache. Keep a water bottle with you at work and sip frequently. The apple juice in this snack also counts toward fluid intake, as do milk and noncaffeinated beverages.

Dinner: 7:00 P.M.

Beef-tofu stir fry: (3 ounces lean beef, 2 ounces firm tofu, ½ cup
    broccoli, ½ cup mixed red and green peppers, 1½ tsp. sesame oil,
    1 tsp. soy sauce, 1½ cups rice)

Salad (1 cup romaine lettuce, 2 tsp. salad dressing)

Apple crisp with walnuts and raisins (½ cup)

Total calories: 1,000

Dinner includes lots of veggies, some protein (from beef and tofu) and carbohydrate from the rice to fuel tomorrow's ride.

Snack: 9:30 P.M.

Toasted English muffin with peanut butter

Total calories: 275

And that's it: a day's menu with about 3,500 calories (61 percent as carbohydrate, 22 percent as fat) and more than 100 percent of the RDA for all vitamins and minerals. It also meets guidelines for fiber, fruit, and vegetable intake.

27
Winning Tips for Losing Weight

Cycling is great exercise, but it doesn't make you immune to gaining weight. Just ask Jan Ullrich, the young German star who won the 1997 Tour de France. He gained nearly 20 pounds in the winter after his victory, then struggled the next season to get back to racing weight. It took him the entire spring, despite many miles of hard training and racing.

Of course, weight control is a lot easier if you don't get chunky in the first place. If Ullrich had spent more time on winter training and less on the banquet circuit, his metabolism and caloric expenditure would have been higher, keeping those pounds away. One common desperation strategy—an ultra-low-calorie crash diet—is simply out of the question for cyclists. It leaves you too weak to ride well, which is certain to undermine motivation.

Maybe you're not in the running for this year's Tour, but if you'd like to get rid of excess weight in a way that also makes you fitter for cycling, use this two-pronged approach: Eat smarter, and rev up your exercise program. Here's the right way—and the wrong way—to do it.

Don't: starve yourself. If you want to keep riding well, you need the strength and stamina that only come from enough carbohydrate and protein. And if you're hungry all the time, you're much more likely to give in to cravings for high-calorie foods.

Do: eat foods that make you feel full with fewer calories. Legumes, whole grains, fruits and vegetables, along with extra lean meat, poultry, and fish, are among the most nutritious foods you can eat. They're also more likely to satisfy your hunger even when you eat less.

Don't: follow a hardcore diet. You may have friends who lost weight on some high-protein, low-fat, or no-carbo diet, but this doesn't mean it will work for you (or even for your friends after a couple of months). There are two keys to weight loss: Burn more calories than you consume, and do it in a way that you can maintain for a lengthy period. If you eat like most people (and you aren't doing high-intensity training), it won't hurt to cut down on fat and total calories. But don't eat so little that it makes you feel weak or miserable.

Do: track your daily calorie consumption. Use a book that includes every kind of food and mentions brand names, such as *The Complete Book of Food Counts* by Corinne T. Netzer. A computer program makes tracking even easier. Any one that has a large food database will do. If your weight is constant, cutting just 250 calories a day (by eating good foods but reducing portions) will result in the loss of about 2 pounds per month. If you've been gaining weight, cut down more.

Don't: depend entirely on aerobic exercise. Ride hills and add periodic sprints or time trials to your cycling workouts to tax your muscles, boost your heart rate, and increase calorie consumption.

Do: muscle-building exercises. Weight training helps increase your metabolism so you burn more calories even when you're not exercising. It also helps offset the tendency to lose muscle mass along with fat. On the bike, don't subscribe to the popular notion that low-intensity riding burns more fat. The fact is that going harder burns more total calories and is better for weight loss.

Don't: skip meals in an attempt to cut calories. You need to keep your blood sugar steady through the day to sustain your energy level and prevent cravings for high-fat or sweet snacks.

Do: eat numerous small meals per day. These can be the three main meals with snacks between, or five or six meals of the same size. This manner of eating provides a constant supply of energy and reduces your urge to eat big meals that overload your system.

Don't: eat less without riding more. A study of people who successfully lost weight and kept it off for several years found that nearly all of them increased activity levels while they reduced calories.

Do: ride your bike an extra half-hour every day. Although the number of calories burned is dependent on your metabolism and workout intensity, you can easily consume an extra 250 a day this way, resulting in the loss of 2 pounds per month—a healthful rate that's easy to sustain.

Don't: set your goals too high. Trying to lose 20 pounds in a month isn't just difficult, it's unhealthy. And trying to reach such a goal by suddenly quadrupling your mileage is a quick route to injury.

Do: set fitness goals that have nothing to do with weight loss. When members of a New York health center trained to run a marathon, those who did it to improve performance lost weight, while those who did it only because they wanted to lose weight tended to drop out and keep the weight on. So, set a goal that will take several months to reach—completing a century, for example, or an all-day mountain bike ride. Motivation will be even higher if you get friends to commit to the goal with you.

28
Cycling Calorie Counter

How many calories did you burn on today's ride? It's a simple question that, until now, was hard to answer with much precision. Granted, you could estimate your caloric consumption according to averages based on weight and speed. But the results were general and didn't account for all the factors that can affect cycling.

This chapter will change that. For the first time, you'll be able to calculate how many calories you burn on a specific ride. By factoring in terrain, wind, riding position, and drafting, as well as speed and body weight, you'll arrive at the best estimation of caloric expenditure ever devised for cyclists. If you're counting calories as a way to maintain or lose weight, this is your formula for success.

A New Method

Calories are stores of energy contained within the three main food compounds—carbohydrate, fat, and protein. Your body breaks down these compounds and uses a portion of the resulting energy to power the basic physiological processes of life. Simply put, you burn calories just being alive. In fact, during normal daily activities, the rate is about 0.01 calorie per pound of body weight per minute. So if you weigh 150 pounds, you burn approximately 1.5 calories per minute, or 2,160 calories in 24 hours.

The remainder of the energy is either stored as body weight or used to contract muscles for additional movement or exercise. The choice is yours. Accumulate about 3,500 unused calories, for instance, and you'll gain 1 pound. But if you ride regularly, your body will consume these extra calories for energy.

During any aerobic exercise, oxygen is required for caloric combustion. Specifically, 1 liter of oxygen is used for every 5 calories burned. Thus, the way physiology labs have traditionally estimated caloric expenditure is by measuring the amount of oxygen consumed.

James Hagberg, Ph.D., and his colleagues at the University of Florida were among the first to take this understanding out of the laboratory and into the real world. Using mobile equipment, they studied the caloric expenditures of cyclists on the road. Now, using their formula and a calculator, you can put this information to work for you.

Your Starting Point

First, consult "Baseline Values" to determine your starting point. It's the number that appears where your weight and speed intersect. For instance, if you weigh 150 pounds and averaged 15 mph on the ride you're analyzing, then your baseline value is 8.4. Later, you'll add and subtract from this number depending on the factors that influenced your ride.

Baseline Values

SPEED (MPH)	COEFFICIENT (CAL/LB/MIN)	CALORIE EXPENDITURE		
		120 LB	130 LB	140 LB
8	0.0295	3.5	3.8	4.1
10	0.0355	4.3	4.6	5.0
12	0.0426	5.1	5.5	6.0
14	0.0512	6.1	6.7	7.2
15	0.0561	6.7	7.3	7.9
16	0.0615	7.4	8.0	8.6
17	0.0675	8.1	8.8	9.5
18	0.0740	8.9	9.6	10.4
19	0.0811	9.7	10.5	11.4
20	0.0891	10.7	11.6	12.5
21	0.0975	11.7	12.7	13.7
23	0.1173	14.1	15.1	16.4
25	0.1411	16.9	18.3	19.8

If you pedaled at a fairly constant rate throughout the ride, then average speed is suitable for computing baseline value. If there were parts where your speed increased or decreased significantly, however, divide the ride into several portions and calculate each segment separately. For instance, on a 3-hour ride, 1 hour might have been spent at 20 mph, another at 18 mph, and a third at 16 mph. Although the average speed is 18 mph, you actually burned more calories than if you had maintained this rate throughout.

The reason is simple. As you go faster, air resistance and energy expenditure increase exponentially. Raising your speed 2 mph for 60 minutes gives you a calorie-burning boost that's not entirely offset by decreasing your speed 2 mph for the same period.

Once you have your baseline value, write it on line 1 of the Calorie Consumption Worksheet on page 104. Now it's time to adjust this number based on some key variables.

		CALORIE EXPENDITURE			
150 LB	160 LB	170 LB	180 LB	190 LB	200 LB
4.4	4.7	5.0	5.3	5.6	5.9
5.3	5.7	6.0	6.4	6.7	7.1
6.4	6.8	7.2	7.7	8.1	8.5
7.7	8.2	8.7	9.2	9.7	10.2
8.4	9.0	9.5	10.1	10.7	11.2
9.2	9.8	10.5	11.1	11.7	12.3
10.1	10.8	11.5	12.2	12.8	13.5
11.1	11.8	12.6	13.3	14.1	14.8
12.2	13.0	13.8	14.6	15.4	16.2
13.4	14.3	15.1	16.0	16.9	17.8
14.6	15.6	16.6	17.6	18.5	19.5
17.6	18.8	19.9	21.1	22.3	23.5
21.2	22.6	24.0	25.4	26.8	28.2

NOTE: If your weight is not listed in the table, determine your baseline value by multiplying your weight (in pounds) by the coefficient next to your speed. For instance, if you weigh 165 pounds and rode 17 mph, multiply 165 by 0.0675. The result (11.1) is your baseline value.

Surface Area

Air resistance is the biggest obstacle to overcome while riding. An important factor is your surface area—the size of the body you're trying to move through the air. The ideal is to be strong and lean. This way you have lots of muscle to move minimal surface area.

One study, conducted by *Bicycling* Fitness Advisory Board member David Swain, Ph.D., quantified the effects of size and surface area. He found that for every pound of body weight greater than 154 pounds, energy expenditure per pound decreased by approximately 0.5 percent. Conversely, caloric expenditure increased by the same amount for every pound less than 154. This means that, in most cases, heavier riders can generate more power relative to their body weight. They require less energy than lighter riders to overcome air resistance.

To apply this to yourself, calculate the difference between your weight and 154. Halve this difference, then divide by 100. Multiply the resulting number by your baseline value to derive your surface area adjustment. Write it on line 1a of the Calorie Consumption Worksheet.

Calorie Consumption Worksheet

Line 1: Baseline Value ± _____

Line 1a: Surface Area Adjustment ± _____

Line 2: ± _____

Line 2a: Terrain Adjustment ± _____

Line 3: = _____

Line 3a: Wind Adjustment ± _____

Line 4: = _____

Line 4a: Riding Position Adjustment + _____

Line 5: = _____

Line 5a: Drafting Adjustment − _____

Grand Totals: Total Calories Burned per Minute ± _____

Total Calories Used for Life Support − _____

Total Minutes of Riding × _____

Total Calories Burned Riding = _____

If you weigh more than 154 pounds, subtract this adjustment from your baseline value. If you weigh less, add it. Put the result on line 2.

Terrain

If your ride was mostly flat, put 0 on line 2a and write the same number on line 3 that you did on line 2. Then go to the next section. If your ride was hilly, read on.

Climbing at any speed burns more calories than cycling on flat ground at the same rate. Conversely, when you're descending (even if you pedal) you burn fewer calories than riding on the flats at the same rate. So the question arises, do downhills offset uphills?

For most hilly rides, the calories used while climbing and the calories saved when descending almost offset each other, but not quite. So, if you rode a hilly out-and-back course, an adjustment is necessary. The reason is that as you climb, you're battling gravity. But as you descend, you don't enjoy the full advantage of this force. Once again, air resistance is to blame because it rises exponentially with speed, making the descent not as quick and easy as the climb is slow and hard.

To derive an accurate measure of caloric expenditure, you need to estimate what percentage of the ride was spent climbing. Then multiply your adjusted baseline value (line 2) by 0.01 for each 10 percent. For example, if you were climbing 30 percent of the time, multiply by 0.03. The result is your terrain adjustment. Write it on line 2a and add it to line 2. The sum goes on line 3.

Of course, not every ascent culminates in a descent. A point-to-point ride may have an overall elevation gain. If this describes the ride you're analyzing, multiply your weight by the total number of feet you climbed. The resulting number is in foot/pounds, a measure of work. Thus, if you weigh 150 pounds and took an hour to complete a course with a net elevation gain of 100 feet, you've done 15,000 (150×100) foot/pounds of work. (For precision in measuring vertical gain, the Cateye AT100 cyclecomputer has an altimeter.)

One foot/pound of work requires 0.0014 calories, so multiply the result by this number, then divide by the total minutes ridden. Using the same example, the result is 0.35 calorie per minute ([$15,000 \times 0.0014$] = 21 divided by 60 minutes). This is the number of extra calories required per minute to climb the additional 100 feet. Put the result of your calculations on line 2a, add it to line 2, and write the sum on line 3.

If you rode a point-to-point course that has an overall decrease in elevation, follow the same steps but subtract the result from line 2.

Wind

If you rode in calm conditions, skip this section, write 0 on line 3a, and bring down the previous adjusted baseline value to line 4. If it was windy, however, you'll need to make an adjustment.

Wind, like hills, can make a ride harder or easier. With out-and-back or loop courses, the energy saved with a tailwind almost offsets the extra calories burned against a headwind. However, wind direction varies. Sometimes the headwind you battle on the ride out isn't equal to the tailwind you enjoy on the way back, or vice versa. If the wind changed in this manner during your ride, multiply the adjusted baseline value (line 3) by 0.03 (if the wind was light), 0.04 (if it was moderate), or 0.05 (if it was strong). Write the result on line 3a. If the wind was against you most of the way, add it to the adjusted baseline value on line 3. If it was with you, subtract it.

If you rode a point-to-point course with either a constant headwind or tailwind, you need to make a different adjustment. First, halve the wind speed. If it was a headwind, add this number to your actual speed. If it was a tailwind, subtract it. The result is your wind-adjusted speed. Next, refer again to "Baseline Values" on page 102 and find the number that corresponds to the intersection of your weight and wind-adjusted speed. Subtract your original baseline value (line 1) from this number. The result is your wind adjustment, which should be entered on line 3a. Again, if you had a headwind, it should be added to line 3. If you had a tailwind, it should be subtracted. Tally the result on line 4.

So, if you weigh 150 pounds and rode 15 mph into a 10-mph headwind, your wind-adjusted speed is 20 mph (10 divided by 2 + 15) and your wind adjustment is 5 (13.4 [adjusted baseline value] – 8.4 [original baseline value]). Since it was a headwind, the result is added to line 3. Conversely, if you weigh 150 pounds and rode 15 mph with a 10-mph tailwind, your wind adjustment is 3.1 (8.4 – 5.3), which is subtracted from line 3.

Wind conditions are rarely this distinct, however. A crosswind is more common than a direct headwind or tailwind. The energy requirement of riding with most crosswinds is about 70 percent that of cycling into a headwind. To figure your wind adjustment in a crosswind, use the method described earlier, just as if you had ridden into a headwind. Then multiply the wind adjustment by 0.7 and add the result to the adjusted baseline value.

If you weigh 150 pounds and rode 15 mph in a 10-mph crosswind, your wind adjustment is 3.5 (5 × 0.7). Add this to line 3.

Riding Position

At speeds below 15 mph, there's little difference between the caloric cost of riding in an upright position or low on the drops or on an aero bar. However, when you're moving faster, a low position burns significantly fewer calories. Similarly, you expend less energy when your bike is free of racks, panniers, fenders, and so on, all of which make you less aerodynamic.

If you were in a low position for most of the ride, you don't need to adjust your baseline value. Simply enter the same number on line 5 that you did on line 4. But if you sat upright most of the time, or if your bike was outfitted with panniers, consult "Riding Position Adjustment." Find your speed and the increase in caloric expenditure listed beside it. Multiply your adjusted baseline value (line 4) by this number, then enter the result on line 4a. Add it to line 4 and write the sum on line 5.

Drafting

Dr. Hagberg's research found that drafting reduces workload by about 1 percent for each mph.

If you didn't draft, or if you rode alone, no adjustment is necessary

Riding Position Adjustment

SPEED (MPH)	INCREASES IN CALORIE EXPENDITURE
15	03
16	08
17	12
18	18
19	22
20	26
22.5	38
25	50

on your worksheet. But if you drafted another cyclist for the entire ride, you need to turn your speed into a percentage and subtract it from the adjusted baseline value (line 5). For instance, if you rode at 15 mph, take 15 percent of your adjusted baseline value. Write the result on line 5a and subtract it from line 5.

It's more likely, however, that you drafted for only part of the ride. If so, convert your speed from mph to percent as before. Then estimate what fraction of the ride you drafted and, in turn, take that percentage of your adjusted baseline value. For example, if you drafted for a third of a 15-mph ride, take 5 percent (⅓ of 15) of line 5. Enter the result on line 5a, then subtract it from line 5. This gives you the total number of calories burned per minute of riding.

Final Adjustment

Because this result includes your body's basic physiological requirements for living, you need to make one final adjustment to determine how many calories were used just for riding.

Multiply your weight in pounds by 0.01, which is the number of calories per pound that you burn naturally. Subtract the result from total calories burned per minute. Then multiply by the total minutes of riding. The result is the total calories burned while riding. Then think of all the calories you used just figuring this out.

Anatomy of a Bike

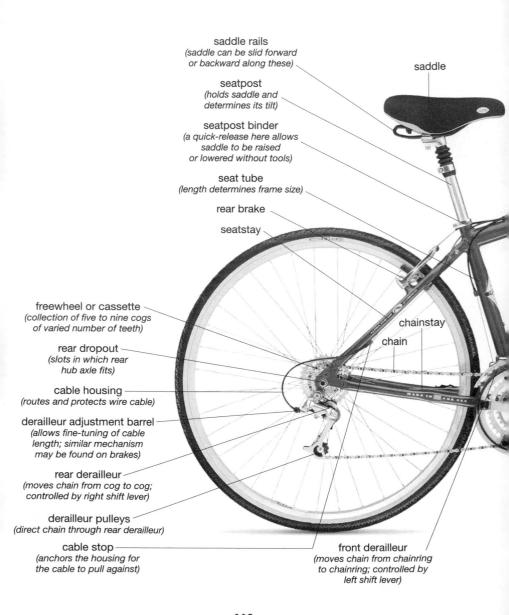

saddle rails
*(saddle can be slid forward
or backward along these)*

saddle

seatpost
*(holds saddle and
determines its tilt)*

seatpost binder
*(a quick-release here allows
saddle to be raised
or lowered without tools)*

seat tube
(length determines frame size)

rear brake

seatstay

freewheel or cassette
*(collection of five to nine cogs
of varied number of teeth)*

chainstay

chain

rear dropout
*(slots in which rear
hub axle fits)*

cable housing
(routes and protects wire cable)

derailleur adjustment barrel
*(allows fine-tuning of cable
length; similar mechanism
may be found on brakes)*

rear derailleur
*(moves chain from cog to cog;
controlled by right shift lever)*

derailleur pulleys
(direct chain through rear derailleur)

cable stop
*(anchors the housing for
the cable to pull against)*

front derailleur
*(moves chain from chainring
to chainring; controlled by
left shift lever)*

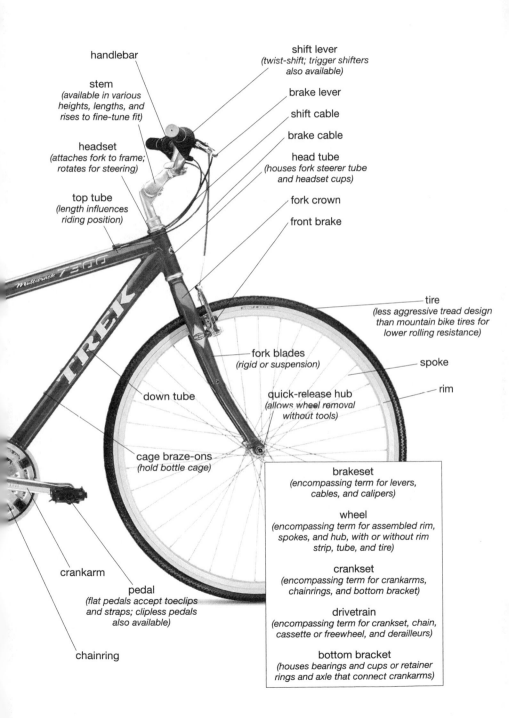

handlebar

shift lever
*(twist-shift; trigger shifters
also available)*

stem
*(available in various
heights, lengths, and
rises to fine-tune fit)*

brake lever

shift cable

headset
*(attaches fork to frame;
rotates for steering)*

brake cable

head tube
*(houses fork steerer tube
and headset cups)*

top tube
*(length influences
riding position)*

fork crown

front brake

tire
*(less aggressive tread design
than mountain bike tires for
lower rolling resistance)*

fork blades
(rigid or suspension)

spoke

down tube

quick-release hub
*(allows wheel removal
without tools)*

rim

cage braze-ons
(hold bottle cage)

brakeset
*(encompassing term for levers,
cables, and calipers)*

wheel
*(encompassing term for assembled rim,
spokes, and hub, with or without rim
strip, tube, and tire)*

crankarm

crankset
*(encompassing term for crankarms,
chainrings, and bottom bracket)*

pedal
*(flat pedals accept toeclips
and straps; clipless pedals
also available)*

drivetrain
*(encompassing term for crankset, chain,
cassette or freewheel, and derailleurs)*

bottom bracket
*(houses bearings and cups or retainer
rings and axle that connect crankarms)*

chainring

Glossary

A

Aerobic: Exercise at an intensity that allows the body's need for oxygen to be continually met. This level of intensity can be sustained for long periods.

Aerodynamic: A design of cycling equipment or a riding position that reduces wind resistance. Aero for short.

Anaerobic: Exercise above the intensity at which the body's need for oxygen can be met. This intensity can be sustained only briefly.

B

Bonk: A state of severe exhaustion caused mainly by the depletion of glycogen in the muscles because the rider has failed to eat or drink enough. Once it occurs, rest and high-carbohydrate foods are necessary for recovery.

Bottom bracket: The part of the frame where the crankset is installed. Also the axle, cups, and bearings of the crankset.

BPM: Abbreviation for beats per minute in reference to heart rate.

C

Cadence: The number of times during 1 minute that a pedal stroke is completed. Also called pedal rpm.

Carbohydrate: In the diet it is broken down into glucose, the body's principal energy source, through digestion and metabolism. It is stored as glycogen in the liver and muscles. Carbo can be simple (sugars) or complex (bread, pasta, grains, fruits, vegetables), which contains additional nutrients. One gram of carbohydrate supplies 4 calories.

Cardiovascular: Pertaining to the heart and blood vessels.

Cassette: The set of gear cogs on the rear hub. Also called a freewheel, cluster, or block.

Century: A 100-mile ride. A metric century is 100 kilometers.

Chondromalacia: A serious knee injury in which there is disintegration of cartilage surfaces due to improper tracking of the kneecap. Symptoms start with deep knee pain and a crunching sensation when bending.

Cleat: A metal or plastic fitting on the sole of a cycling shoe that engages the pedal.

Cog: A sprocket on the rear wheel's cassette or freewheel.

Crash rash: Any skin abrasion resulting from a fall. Also called road rash.

Criterium: A mass-start race covering numerous laps of a course that is normally about 1 mile or less in length.

Cross-training: Combining sports for mental refreshment and physical conditioning, especially during cycling's off season.

Crunches: An exercise for abdominal muscles. Lie on your back with knees bent 90 degrees and feet flat. Rest hands on chest. Curl your torso upward, keeping the lower back on floor. Hold briefly, lower slowly, repeat.

D

Downshift: To shift to a lower gear, such as a larger cog or smaller chainring.

Drafting: Riding closely behind another rider to take advantage of the windbreak (slipstream) and use about 20 percent less energy. Also called sitting in or wheelsucking.

Drops: The lower part of a down-turned handlebar typically found on a road bike. The curved portions are called the hooks.

E

Electrolytes: Substances such as sodium, potassium, and chloride that are necessary for muscle contraction and maintenance of fluid levels.

Ergometer: A stationary, bicycle-like device with adjustable pedal resistance used in physiological testing or for indoor training.

F

Fat: In the diet it is the most concentrated source of food energy, supplying 9 calories per gram. Stored fat provides about half the energy required for low-intensity exercise.

G

Glucose: A sugar, glucose in the bloodstream is the only fuel that can be used by the brain.

Glutes: The gluteal muscles of the buttocks. They are key to pedaling power.

Glycogen: A fuel derived as glucose (sugar) from carbohydrate and stored in the muscles and liver. It's the primary energy source for high-intensity cycling. Reserves are normally depleted after about 2½ hours of riding.

Glycogen window: The period within an hour after exercise when depleted muscles are most receptive to restoring their glycogen content. By eating foods or drinking fluids rich in carbohydrate, energy stores and recovery are enhanced.

Gorp: Good ol' raisins and peanuts, a high-energy mix for nibbling during rides. Can also include nuts, seeds, M&Ms, or granola.

H

Hammer: To ride strongly in big gears.

Hamstrings: The muscles on the backs of the thighs; not well-developed by cycling.

Headset: The parts at the top and bottom of the frame's head tube, into which the handlebar stem and fork are fitted.

I

Intervals: A structured method of training that alternates brief, hard efforts with short periods of easier riding for partial recovery.

J

Jam: A period of hard, fast riding.

Jump: A quick, hard acceleration.

L

Lactate threshold (LT): The exertion level beyond which the body can no longer produce energy aerobically, resulting in the buildup of lactic acid. This is marked by muscle fatigue, pain, and shallow, rapid breathing. Also called anaerobic threshold (AT).

Lactic acid: A substance formed during anaerobic metabolism when there is incomplete breakdown of glucose. It rapidly produces muscle fatigue and pain. Also called lactate.

LSD: Long, steady distance. A training technique that requires a firm aerobic pace for at least 2 hours.

M

Mass start: Events such as road races, cross-country races, and criteriums in which all contestants leave the starting line at the same time.

Max VO₂: The maximum amount of oxygen that can be consumed during all-out exertion. This is a key indicator of a person's potential in cycling and other aerobic sports. It's largely genetically determined but can be improved somewhat by training.

O

Orthotics: Custom-made supports worn in shoes to help neutralize biomechanical imbalances in the feet or legs.

Overtraining: Deep-seated fatigue, both physical and mental, caused by training at an intensity or volume too great for adaptation.

P

Paceline: A group formation in which each rider takes a turn breaking the wind at the front before pulling off, dropping to the rear position, and riding the others' draft until at the front once again.

Panniers: Large bike bags used by touring cyclists or commuters. Panniers attach to racks that place them low on each side of the rear wheel, and sometimes the front wheel.

Power: The combination of speed and strength.

Protein: In the diet it is required for tissue growth and repair. Composed of structural units called amino acids, protein is not a significant energy source unless not enough calories and carbohydrate are consumed. One gram of protein equals 4 calories.

Pusher: A rider who pedals in a large gear at a relatively slow cadence, relying on the gear size for speed.

Q

Quadriceps: The large muscle in front of the thigh, the strength of which helps determine a cyclist's ability to pedal with power. Quads for short.

R

Reach: The combined length of a bike's top tube and stem, which determines the rider's distance to the handlebar.

Repetition: Each hard effort in an interval workout. Also, one complete movement in a weight-training exercise. Rep for short.

Resistance trainer: A stationary training device into which the bike is clamped. Pedaling resistance increases with pedaling speed to simulate actual riding. Also known as an indoor, wind, or mag trainer (the last two names derived from the fan or magnet that creates resistance on the rear wheel).

Rise: The upward angle (if any) of a handlebar stem.

Rollers: An indoor training device consisting of three or four long cylinders connected by belts. Both bike wheels roll on these cylinders so that balancing is much like actual riding.

S

Saddle sores: Skin problems in the crotch that develop from chafing caused by pedaling action. Sores can range from tender raw spots to boil-like lesions if infection occurs.

Saddle time: Time spent cycling.

Set: In intervals or weight training, a specific number of repetitions.

Singletrack: A trail so narrow that two cyclists can't easily ride side by side, which makes passing difficult or impossible.

Speed: The ability to accelerate quickly and maintain a very fast cadence for brief periods.

Speedwork: A general term for intervals and other high-velocity training, such as sprints, time trials, and motorpacing.

Spin: To pedal at high cadence.

Spinner: A rider who pedals in a moderate gear at a relatively fast cadence, relying on pedal rpm for speed.

T

Time trial (TT): A race against the clock in which individual riders start at set intervals and cannot give or receive a draft. In training, an extended period of riding at near-maximum effort.

Tops: The part of a drop handlebar between the stem and the brake levers.

U

Upshift: To shift to a higher gear, that is, a smaller cog or larger chainring.

Index

Boldface page references indicate photographs and illustrations.
Underscored references indicate boxed text.

A

Abdominal crunch, 54–55, 69–70, **70**
Abrasions, 13, 78, 85
Accelerating, 17
Accessories, 4
Achilles tendinitis, 77–78
Aero bar, 15
Aerobic activities, 55, 61, 101–2. *See also specific types*
Aging, stretching and, 79
Ailments and injuries, 13, 65–69, 74–78, 79, 84–87
Air resistance, 104–5
Anatomy of bike, **114–15**
Ankle ailments and soreness, 77–78
Antibiotic gel, 72
Antioxidants, 22

B

Back
  soreness, 69–71, **70**, 74
  stretching, 81
Bag Balm, 72
Banana, 92
Baseline values, 102, 102–3
Basics, cycling, 12–14
Bath treatment, 42, 73
Beater bike, 27
Bench press, 54
Bleeding, heavy, 84–85
Boils, 73
Bonking, 91
Breakfast, 94
Burn pad, nonstick moist, 73
Buttocks ailments, 76–77. *See also* Saddle sores, preventing
Buying a new bike, 3–6

C

Caffeine, 41, 92
Calcium, 94
Calorie counter, cycling, 101–8, 102–3, 104, 107
Calves, stretching, 80
Camps, cycling, 28
Cancer, skin, 78
Carbo gels, 95
Carbohydrates, 92, 95
Chafing, 13, 76–77
Chain lube, dry, 28
Chamois Butt'r, 13, 71–72
Children, cycling with, 28–29
Chondromalacia, 68
City streets, cycling on, 12
Cleat alignment, **7**, 8–9, 66–67
Clothing, cycling, 13, 27, 71
Coach, for cycling, 28
Collarbone, broken, 85–86
Commitment to cycling, 45
Commuting, 29
Consciousness, loss of, 84
Contusion, 78
Cool down, 13, 44, 56
Cornering, 17
CPR, 84
Cramps, muscle, 76, 91–92
Crashes, first-aid for, 83–87, 86
Crash rash, 85
Cross-country skiing, 55
Cross-training, 34–35, 55
Crunch, abdominal, 54–55, 69–70, **70**

D

Dehydration, preventing, 91. *See also* Hydration
Diary, cycling, 42

119